THE PAULINE RENAISSANCE
IN ENGLAND

THE
Pauline Renaissance
in England

PURITANISM AND THE BIBLE

BY

JOHN S. COOLIDGE

CLARENDON PRESS · OXFORD

1970

Oxford University Press, Ely House, London W.1

GLASGOW   NEW YORK   TORONTO   MELBOURNE   WELLINGTON
CAPE TOWN   SALISBURY   IBADAN   NAIROBI   DAR ES SALAAM   LUSAKA   ADDIS ABABA
BOMBAY   CALCUTTA   MADRAS   KARACHI   LAHORE   DACCA
KUALA LUMPUR   SINGAPORE   HONG KONG   TOKYO

MADE AND PRINTED IN GREAT BRITAIN BY
WILLIAM CLOWES AND SONS, LIMITED
LONDON AND BECCLES

TO MY WIFE
CAROLYN

PREFACE

THIS study attempts to define Puritanism as an episode in that powerful reapprehension and development of biblical thought which constitutes the Reformation as an era of intellectual history. It centres on the Puritan understanding of Christian liberty, arguing that this is what originally distinguishes Puritanism from Elizabethan Conformity. The Puritans' expositions of the combined Pauline imperatives of liberty and edification illustrate the best sense of their insistence on scriptural authority and describe their conception of the living Church. This study traces the development of that conception and its complication with another, equally Pauline but apparently antithetical idea of the Church; and this essential conflict of Puritan ecclesiology is seen in relation to the comprehensive dialectic of Paul's thought as elaborated in the Covenant Theology.

In that this study attempts to follow Puritan thought through successive phases, it is an essay in history. However, it has no contribution to make to factual knowledge of the history of the Elizabethan Puritan movemant and its sequels, for which I have relied on authorities in the Bibliography, and I have eschewed historical narrative. Neither have I attempted to describe all aspects of Puritan exegetic practice; my primary documents are almost all polemical tracts or treatises, in which large questions of interpretation governing the evolution of Puritanism can most obviously be traced. Finally, while I have attempted to assess Calvin's relation to English Puritan thought on some important points, I have not generally pursued the search for Continental antecedents. My tentative impression is that it would not yield much in respect of the principal matters discussed here. For example, the topics of Christian liberty and edification do not appear to figure in Continental Anabaptists' arguments for separation; and the ambiguity of Covenant 'conditions' seems to occupy the attention of English exponents of Federal Theology much more than it does that of their Continental mentors. The impression of independent development which is conveyed by treating Puritan thought as I have done seems to me essentially true. Such, then, are the intentional limitations of this study.

In order not to give an adventitious appearance of quaintness to those writers whose works are not quoted from modernized editions, spelling and punctuation in such quotations are modernized here. Italics in the original text which are clearly intended to signify only that words and phrases are being quoted from an opponent's work are not reproduced here unless that fact is relevant to the present discussion. Sources of quotations and other references are indicated by figures in footnotes or in parentheses in the text: the first number is that of the item as listed in the Bibliography; it is followed by page reference(s) or the equivalent. References to Calvin's *Institutes* and to Hooker's *Laws of Ecclesiastical Polity* are further identified by book, chapter, and section. A few works which are referred to in connection with particular points but are not basically germane to this study have not been placed in the Bibliography; these are identified in footnotes.

I have been assisted by two grants from the University of California and by a Grant-in-Aid from the Huntington Library.

Berkeley   J.S.C.
March. 1970

CONTENTS

INTRODUCTION   xi

I. SCRIPTURAL AUTHORITY   1

II. CHRISTIAN LIBERTY AND EDIFICATION   23

III. SEPARATION   55

IV. FROM GENERATION TO GENERATION   77

V. THE COVENANT OF GRACE   99

VI. THE PAULINE RENAISSANCE   141

BIBLIOGRAPHY   152

INDEX   159

INTRODUCTION

ENGLISH Puritanism brings into clearest definition that aspect of the Reformation which Max Weber has described as the logical conclusion of 'that great historic process in the development of religions, the elimination of magic from the world'.[1] The Puritan movement began in a situation in which the large doctrinal conquests of the Reformation could be considered secure. It concerned doctrinal matters, at the beginning, only indirectly, in that it claimed to see a treacherous inconsistency between the doctrine of the English Church and its ceremonial accoutrements; and that inconsistency was seen as a voluntary retardation of, quite precisely, Weber's 'Entzauberung der Welt': 'They are strangely bewitched, I say, that will bind their English priesthood and sacraments to garments: but much more enchanted, that can find no garments to please them, but such as have been openly polluted with Popery, superstition, and Idolatry.'[2] For Puritans the Gospel has a power like that of Arthur's bright shield in *The Faerie Queene*:

> No magicke arts hereof had any might,
> Nor bloudie wordes of bold Enchaunters call,
> But all that was not such, as seemd in sight,
> Before that shield did fade, and suddeine fall . . .
> (I. vii. 35).

This militant disenchantment cannot be unrelated to other historic factors tending to dispel whatever sacral aura had seemed to invest man's relations to his social environment as well as to his natural one. Just as the 'scenic apparatus' which Elizabeth required her churchmen to maintain sometimes chagrined the most loyal of them,[3] so her pageantry of state must sometimes have required a willing suspension of the age's real sense of the nature

---

[1] 118, 105. [2] 84, 13.

[3] 'The scenic apparatus of divine worship is now under agitation [Agitur nunc de sacro et scenico apparatu]; and those very things which you and I have so often laughed at, are now seriously and solemnly entertained by certain persons, (for *we* are not consulted) as if the Christian religion could not exist without something tawdry [quasi religio Christiana constare non possit sine pannis].' John Jewel to Peter Martyr in *The Zurich Letters* (93, 23).

of things. Both suggest an anxiety as characteristic of the age as its expansive energies. Shakespeare's Richard II, who has been called his representative of 'sacramental man',[4] tells his queen at their parting:

> Learn, good soul,
> To think our former state a happy dream;
> From which awak'd, the truth of what we are
> Shows us but this.
>
> (v. i. 17–20.)

'Though for no other cause, yet for this,' Richard Hooker begins his monumental work, 'that posterity may know we have not loosely through silence permitted things to pass away as in a dream...'[5] Elizabethan Englishmen felt premonitions of an era which would one day come to be described by men of a very different cast of mind in terms reminiscent of theirs: 'All that is solid melts into the air, all that is holy is profaned, and man is at last compelled to face with sober senses his real conditions of life and his relations with his kind.'[6]

Puritans pressed forward into this wilderness, appallingly eager, it has sometimes seemed to their posterity, to discard whatever might 'keep the memory of Egypt still amongst us'.[7] The reason is not only that, as Weber and others have observed, the religion of ancient Israel marks a decisive stage in the 'elimination of magic from the world', and widespread reading of the biblical account of that process prompted a resumption of it. More significantly, this Bible-reading was itself an exodus, an emergence out of a realm of images into a new kind of apprehension of meaning. 'If Bible-reading tended to overstress the Old Testament,' A. G. Dickens remarks, 'it also popularized Pauline theology, that intellectual element of the faith which could not have been spread abroad by the theatrical modes of presentation used by the medieval Church upon a less literate public.'[8] One ingenuous apologist for the disputed ceremonies and vestments argues that 'simple souls are as well fed with seeing as hearing, so much the better as

---

[4] John Dover Wilson uses this phrase in the Introduction to his edition of the play (Cambridge, England, 1939), p. xvii, attributing it to Hilaire Belloc.
[5] 57.
[6] *The Communist Manifesto*, I, 'Bourgeois and Proletarians'.
[7] 42, 35.
[8] 33, 137.

nature hath more sufficiently enabled them by outward sense to discern the one, than knowledge, skill, or experience to judge of the other'.[9] As simple souls came to read and to hear biblical texts explicated from the pulpit and in those exciting seminars called 'prophesyings', they might well feel the old modes of presentation as a form of bondage. They were not left desolate by the passing from the world of so much that had seemed instinct with numinous value, because their lives were informed in a new way.

The present study attempts to describe that way. It argues that Puritanism originates as a response to elements of Pauline theology which are especially pertinent to a time of cultural dislocation, that English Separatism and Congregationalism are further developments of Paul's complex ecclesiology—or, as it may be useful to call it, his sociology of life in Christ—and that a Pauline understanding of scripture is in fact the matrix of Puritan thought generally.

To seek the main source of the Puritans' thought where they themselves insisted it was to be found is something of a 'new and original plan' for modern Puritan studies. The great epoch of the study of Puritan intellectual history which was brought about to an extraordinary extent by the work of the late Perry Miller began at a time when, apparently, the Bible itself could hardly be thought of as anything but a cultural incubus. Even biblical scholarship had some appearance of demolishing it. H. H. Rowley recalls that when he began his theological studies 'it would have seemed a hazardous thing to announce a course of lectures on the Unity of the Bible. The emphasis then was predominantly on the diversity of the Bible, and such a title ... would have involved some suspicion that the author was an out-of-date obscurantist.'[10] Diversity alone is meaningless, and the historian of Puritanism might crudely suppose modern scholarship to have shown that anyone who had ever thought he saw consequential meaning in the Bible was necessarily deceiving himself. 'Since historical Biblical scholarship was practically non-existent,' Miller explains, 'a man's personal reaction to the cryptic utterances of the Word was bound to be his ultimate criterion of what they signified.'[11] The truism that so large and various a book can supply proof texts for just about any persuasion could be assumed to apply in a special sense to the druidical

[9] 62, 44. [10] 99. 15. [11] 73, 75.

miscellany that Miller's phrase suggests. However, as Rowley says, 'a very considerable change of climate has come over Biblical studies' since that time.[12] Not that the diversity and conflict which earlier scholars emphasized has been called into question, but a new appreciation has developed of 'a more profoundly significant unity running through it all'.[13] It is not the unity of a monolith but that of a *discordia concors*, precisely the kind of dynamic unity in diversity which aesthetic theory and literary criticism ever since the Romantic period have valued above all else; and it is especially characteristic of that part of the Bible from which Puritans learned how to interpret the whole, the Epistles of Paul. 'Paul is a man of antitheses and contradictions,' Hans Joachim Schoeps has said; 'his thought could attain harmony only through dialectics and antinomies. But should he not perhaps appeal in this very respect to the modern consciousness?'[14] While the Puritans by no means anticipate the methods or findings of scientific criticism, it will be argued here that the lines of force which Paul's teaching and their own experience make them aware of in the Bible correspond significantly to lines of historical development that have come to be discernible in and behind the biblical record. Puritanism renews the complex development of personal and historical religious experience which has been called 'the biblical process'.[15]

---

[12] 99, 16.   [13] 99, 17.   [14] 103, 278.

[15] E. A. Speiser, Introduction to The Anchor Bible *Genesis* (110, xliii–lii). Cf. Rowley (99, 26–7): 'Whenever we approach the Bible, and especially the Old Testament, which covers so long a period of time, we must maintain a historical sense, and read everything first of all in the setting of its own age and then in the context of the whole unfolding revelation of which it forms a part. The unity is the unity of a process and a development. Within the unity of a man's personality there is growth and development. The ideas of his youth are not identical with the ideas of advancing age; yet neither are they wholly different and unrelated. A continuing thread runs through them, and though there may be modification there is not a continual new beginning. The moments are fleeting and the experience of today will be gone tomorrow. Yet not wholly. By memory the experience of the past is retained in some measure, and there is a deposit in the stuff of personality of the things through which a man has lived. Moreover, the effects of his will are seen in his personality. The things he has chosen to do have modified his character, and he may have grown better or worse, either continuously or by turns, through the years. The continuing thread that marks the unity of his personality may not be set in a straight line. The unity of the Bible is of this kind, though given in the experience of a people and not in a single life. The experience, character, and will of the persons who mark the successive moments of the process all left their mark on the process. For each moment was more than a moment; it belonged to the whole.'

I

SCRIPTURAL AUTHORITY

JOHN WHITGIFT says in the beginning of his reply to the authors of the Puritan *Admonition to the Parliament* (1572):

> But, before I enter into their reasons, I think it not amiss to examine that assertion which is the chief and principal ground (so far as I can gather) of their book; that is, that 'those things only are to be placed in the church which the Lord himself in his word commandeth.' As though they should say, nothing is to be tolerated in the church of Christ, touching either doctrine, order, ceremonies, discipline, or government, except it be expressed in the word of God.[1]

Like Richard Hooker writing after him and lesser apologists for Conformity before, Whitgift gladly acknowledges that the appeal to scriptural authority is the very life of Puritanism. Whatever else may be said about the Puritan programme is secondary; it will lose its imperative force the moment its proponents are convicted of having 'learned not all the orders prescribed therein out of God's holy word, but somewhat elsewhere'.[2] To Conformists it appeared self-evident that such was the case, and so it has appeared since to nearly all concerned; but what was then regarded as the one fatal charge to make against Puritanism has since come to seem the one necessary presupposition for any attempt to defend it, or even to make it interesting: that the Puritans really derived their convictions from some other source than the Bible. They can be credited appreciatively, if somewhat patronizingly, with an eager response to the 'poetry' of the Bible and an intense preoccupation with the drama of salvation described there, but more convincing sources must be found for their ideas on Church polity, their attitude to the civil authority, and even for their theology, if these are to command respect. In order to argue that Puritanism had a mind, it has seemed necessary to assume that Puritan writers regularly deluded

[1] 120, I, 176.
[2] 10, 56.

themselves by a curious ritual, casting a dust of scriptural references over pages where, nevertheless, an ingenious modern investigator can discover traces of thought.

This supposed deception wrought by the Puritan mind upon itself has been taken to indicate an underlying existential anxiety. Perry Miller puts the case as follows:

> That Protestantism appealed to the authority of the Bible against the authority of the Pope is a platitude of history. That the Calvinists were vehement asserters of its finality is also common knowledge. What is frequently forgotten is that without a Bible, this piety would have confronted chaos. It could not have found guidance in reason, because divine reason is above and beyond the human; not in the church, because God is not committed to preserving the orthodoxy or purity of any institution; not in immediate inspiration, because inward promptings are as apt to come from the Devil as from God; not from experimental science, because providence is arbitrary and unpredictable; not from philosophy, because philosophy arises from the senses, which are deceptive, or from innate ideas, which are corrupted, or from definitions of the attributes, which are mental creations. Unless the formless transcendence consents, at some moment in time, to assume the form of man and to speak 'after an humane manner,' men will have nothing to go upon. In the Bible God has so spoken.[3]

So explained, the peculiar game which the Puritan mind is supposed to have played with itself becomes comprehensible, even impressive, to the modern mind. The apparently compulsive citing of scripture can be seen as a protective device allowing the mind to elaborate a rational system of life and thought, assured—at the price of that one arbitrary irrationality—against the inrush of nihilism.

Such would appear to be the accepted rationale for discussing Puritan thought at length, and with ostensible sympathy and respect, while disregarding its biblical aspect. Historically, however, Puritanism must be defined in the first instance by contradistinction from Anglican Conformity, and historically the 'chief and principal ground' of intellectual difference between Conformists and Puritans concerns the appeal to scriptural authority. Since the grounds on which Conformists object to the Puritan's manner of appealing to scripture seem to make excellent sense to modern readers, no explanation which does not bear on the difference between Conformist and Puritan attitudes toward scripture can really account for what seems strange to the modern mind in the Puritan attitude. To that difference Miller's account is irrelevant. None of the considerations he enumerates distinguishes the Puritan from the Conformist. Both Puritans and Conformists hold that the Bible contains all the knowledge that is necessary for salvation, and they agree that 'this glimmering sight which remaineth in the accursed nature of men'[4] can never find out such knowledge by itself. 'As the light of nature doth cause the mind to apprehend those truths which are merely rational,' Hooker writes, 'so that saving truth, which is far above the reach of human reason, cannot otherwise, than by the Spirit of the Almighty, be conceived.'[5] What Miller says is as true of the Conformist as of the Puritan, therefore, with respect to knowledge necessary for salvation; but with respect to other knowledge it is not true of either. Where knowledge of the nature of things is concerned, or practical prudence, or civil policy, or morality, there is no evidence that the Puritan is any less confident of natural reason and the evidence of the senses than the Conformist. Even in matters of faith and worship the difference between them does not concern the kind of distrust of human perception and reasoning that Miller supposes. 'A number there are,' Hooker says, 'who think they cannot admire as they ought the power and authority of the word of God, if in things divine they should attribute any force to man's reason', and he goes on to list six 'usual and common discourses' employed by his adversaries to 'disgrace reason'; but none of the six has anything to do with scepticism.[6] In short, neither the Puritan nor the Conformist

[4] 17, 101.
[5] 57, III, 516: Sermon II, 26.
[6] 57, I, 365–366: *Laws*, III, viii, 4: 'First, "the natural man perceiveth not the things of the Spirit of God; for they are foolishness unto him: neither can he know them, because they are spiritually discerned' [1 Cor. 2:14]. Secondly, it is not for nothing that St. Paul giveth charge to "beware of philosophy" [Col. 2:8], that is to say, such knowledge as men by natural reason attain unto. Thirdly, consider them that have from time to time opposed themselves against the Gospel of Christ, and most troubled the Church with heresy. Have they not always been great admirers of human reason? Hath their deep and profound skill in secular learning made them the more obedient to the truth, and not armed them rather against it? Fourthly, they that fear God will remember how heavy his sentences are in this case: "I will destroy the wisdom of the wise, and will cast away the understanding of the prudent. Where is the wise? where is the scribe? where is the disputer of this world? hath not God made the wisdom of this world foolishness? Seeing the world by wisdom knew not God in

shows any evidence of feeling that without scripture he would confront 'chaos'; both are well assured that they would confront damnation. The hypothesis of epistemological desperation cannot explain the Puritans' special insistence on scriptural authority.

If we wish to understand the Puritan appeal to scriptural authority, then, we should attend carefully to what Puritans and Conformists say to each other on the subject. Their debate on it could hardly be more authoritatively documented, for it is the central strand running through the Admonition controversy and *The Laws of Ecclesiastical Polity*.

The issue is joined over Whitgift's apparently innocent paraphrase: '"those things only are to be placed in the church which the Lord himself in his word commandeth." As though they should say, nothing is to be tolerated in the church ... except it be expressed in the word of God.' Thomas Cartwright, entering the controversy as the acknowledged champion of the cause set forth in the *Admonition*, quickly cries foul:

Is this to interpret? ... are these of like weight, except it be commanded in the word of God, and except it be expressed in the word of God? Many things are both commanded and forbidden, for which there is no express mention in the word, which are as necessarily to be followed or avoided as those whereof express mention is made. Therefore unless your weights be truer, if I could let it, you should weigh none of my words.[7]

Whitgift seems genuinely puzzled by this distinction:

If you mean that 'many things are commanded or forbidden' in the word, which are not expressed in the word, in my opinion you speak contraries; for how can it be commanded or forbidden in the word, except it be also expressed in the same? ... Howsoever you mean it, it

the wisdom of God, it pleased God by the foolishness of preaching to save believers" [1 Cor. 1:19]. Fifthly, the word of God in itself is absolute, exact, and perfect. The word of God is a two-edged sword [Heb. 4:12]; as for the weapons of natural reason, they are as the armour of Saul [1 Sam. 17:39], rather cumbersome about the soldier of Christ than needful. They are not of force to do that which the Apostles of Christ did by the power of the Holy Ghost: "My preaching," therefore saith Paul, "hath not been in the enticing speech of man's wisdom, but in plain evidence of the Spirit and of power, that your faith might not be in the wisdom of men, but in the power of God" [1 Cor. 2:4]. Sixthly, if I believe the Gospel, there needeth no reasoning about it to persuade me; if I do not believe, it must be the Spirit of God and not the reason of man that shall convert my heart unto him.'

    [7] 120, I, 176.

cannot be true; for there is nothing necessary to eternal life which is not both 'commanded' and 'expressed' in the scripture. I count it 'expressed,' when it is either in manifest words contained in scripture, or thereof gathered by necessary collection.

He concludes, as though hesitant to press so obvious an advantage, 'but, because I think it hath but overslipped you, and that upon better advice you will reform it, therefore I will cease to deal further in it, until I understand more of your meaning.'[8] Cartwright, however, professes to be nonplussed by Whitgift's lack of understanding: 'I answer that I suppose that there was never writer, holy nor profane, that ever spake so; and that it biddeth defiance both to divinity and humanity.'[9]

Far from looking for a multitude of specific directions 'either in manifest words contained in scripture, or thereof gathered by necessary collection', Cartwright considers that the proper bearing of scriptural authority on most ecclesiastical matters is contained in four general rules 'which St. Paul gave in such cases as are not particularly mentioned of in the scripture':

I Cor. x.32   The first, that they offend not any, especially the church of God.
I Cor. xiv.40 The second is . . . that all be done in order and comeliness.
I Cor. xiv.26 The third, that all be done to edifying.
Rom. xiv.6–7   The last, that they be done to the glory of God.

So that you see that those things which you reckon up of the hour, and time, and day of prayer, &c., albeit they be not specified in the scripture, yet they are not left to any to order at their pleasure, or so that they be not against the word of God; but even by and according to the word of God they must be established, and those alone to be taken which do agree best and nearest with these rules before recited.[10]

As Cartwright says, these scriptural directions are anything but specific: 'it is not our question (which the A[nswerer] doth so shamefully affirm) whether the scripture have expressed all external ceremonies &c.'[11] The Puritan categorically denies that he means what Conformists nevertheless persist in suspecting that he means: 'to exact at our hands for every action the knowledge of

---

[8] 120, I, 177–8.
[9] 17, 46.
[10] 120, I, 195.
[11] 17, 82.

some place of Scripture out of which we stand bound to deduce it . . .'.[12] On the contrary, Puritans sometimes make a point of insisting that there is no precise scriptural directive for Church ceremonies, and that these should therefore not be the same in all times and places: 'Yea, Christian liberty in them sometimes is necessary to be testified, because there are many so simple, that they know not the difference between those things that are necessary in the Church, and those that are not of necessity.'[13] These four rules do not literally or by strict logical consequence prescribe what garments should be worn by the ministry, for example; they are only general admonitions, but surely they are to be obeyed. 'And so it is brought to pass (which you think a great absurdity)', Cartwright concludes,

that all things in the church should be appointed according to the word of God: whereby it likewise appeareth that we deny not but certain things are left to the order of the church, because they are of that nature which are varied by times, places, persons, and other circumstances, and so could not at once be set down and established for ever; and yet so left to the order of the church, as that it do nothing against the rules aforesaid.[14]

[12] 57, I, 288: *Laws*, II, i, 2. Evidently mindful that responsible spokesmen for the Puritan position explicitly deny this construction of it, Hooker adds 'as by divers testimonies they seek to enforce', which leaves room for supposing that he refers either to the 'testimonies' of various unschooled enthusiasts or to implications found in various other statements of the responsible spokesmen themselves. Modern scholars have been less guarded in attributing this absurdity to Puritanism. See, for example, F. L. Cross (ed.), *The Oxford Dictionary of the Christian Church* (London, 1958), p. 654 (article on Hooker): The Puritans 'held to the literal following of the Scriptures as an absolute in the sense that whatever was not expressly commanded in Scripture was unlawful . . .'; ibid., p. 1127 (on Puritans): 'They demanded express Scriptural warrant for all the details of public worship . . .'; Perry Miller, *Orthodoxy in Massachusetts* (73, 32): 'The essence of the Puritan contention was that even the minutiae of ecclesiastical practice had been prescribed ages ago by Christ himself, and they were to remain forever unchanged by any man'; (73, 34): 'The Puritan assumption was that the Bible gave explicit instructions, but even the most confident admitted that it had some difficult passages and that many particular cases had to be determined rather by inference than by specific provision;' Hyder E. Rollins and Herschel Baker, *The Renaissance in England: Non-dramatic Prose and Verse of the Sixteenth Century* (Boston, 1954), p. 179: 'Squarely meeting his antagonists' claim that every point of ecclesiastical discipline and ritual should have a specific Scriptural sanction, Hooker enlarges the area of discussion to include principles of reason, natural law, history, and tradition with which he countered the puritans' literalism.'

[13] 43, 121.

[14] 120, I, 195.

Whitgift finds this explanation satisfactory. Indeed, he takes it to be just what he has been contending for all along:

Here now I would gladly know what T.C. hath proved against the thing that I have here written, or how he hath justified the proposition of the Admonition which I have refelled. For the sum of all is this: the authors of the Admonition say that 'those things only are to be placed in the church which God himself in his word commandeth.' This I confess to be true in 'matters of salvation and damnation.' But I say it is untrue in matters of 'ceremonies, rites, orders, discipline, and kind of government;' which, being external matters and alterable, are to be altered and changed, appointed and abrogated, according to time, place, and person; 'so that nothing be done against the word of God.' And T.C. confesseth, . . . that 'certain things are left to the order of the church, because they are of that nature which are varied by times, places, persons, and other circumstances, and so could not at once be set down and established for ever; and yet so left to the order of the church, as that it do nothing against the rules aforesaid.' . . . Now, I pray you, tell me what difference is there in our words?[15]

In their words there is indeed no difference at all. Nothing better illustrates the elusiveness of this controversy than that Cartwright, at this juncture, should formulate the Puritan idea of scriptural authority in words which the Conformist can readily make his own. For it is the basic contention of Conformity, not that the established Church polity is the only one sanctioned by scripture, but on the contrary, that scripture leaves men free to work out any polity which suits their circumstances, so long as they do nothing contrary to the general precepts of the Bible. As John Bridges says in his *Defence of the Government Established in the Church of England* . . . (1587), Conformists can readily admit that the Puritan programme is based on scriptural authority, if what is understood is simply that

it is agreeable, or not contrary to God's holy word. . . . But if that answer may thus serve them, I see not why it may not as well serve us, if we have no other government established, but such as is agreeable and not contrary to the holy word of God, although it be not in his holy word expressly prescribed.[16]

Thus the double negative, 'not contrary to' scripture, becomes the rallying cry of Conformity, and by saying he means only that the

---

[15] 120, I, 284.
[16] 10, 56–7.

Church must do 'nothing against' his four rules from Paul, Cartwright seems to Whitgift to have given the game away.

When Whitgift makes a special point of using the double negative, however, Cartwright finds it unsatisfactory. Whitgift glosses a quotation from Augustine, '"That, if any thing be universally observed of the whole church" (not repugnant to the scriptures), for so he meaneth, "not to keep that, or to reason of that, is madness."' Cartwright objects: 'Concerning your gloss ("if it be not repugnant to the scripture"), . . . it is not enough, because it must be grounded by the scripture. . . .'[17] At this point it occurs to Whitgift that, where the observance of general rules is concerned, there is no logical difference between a double negative and a positive agreement with scripture:

> In matters of order, ceremonies, and government, it is sufficient if they 'be not repugnant to the scripture.' Neither do I think any great difference to be betwixt 'not repugnant to the word of God,' and 'according to the word.'[18]

Precisely because the difference between the two ways of expressing agreement with scripture is negligible, the Church can confidently insist on its way.

With this turn in the debate Whitgift can be said to have discovered the fundamental case for Conformity as it will be masterfully argued by Hooker. The laws of nature, discovered by human reason, are in harmony with scripture, which reveals truths in part transcending but always presupposing them. Therefore all propositions concerning matters not literally prescribed for in the Bible may confidently be assumed to be 'agreeable and not contrary to the holy word of God', so long as they are, as Hooker says,

> . . . framed according to the law of Reason; the general axioms, rules, and principles of which law being so frequent in Holy Scripture, there is no let but in that regard even out of Scripture such duties [as are prescribed on rational grounds] may be deduced by some kind of consequence, (as by long circuit of deduction it may be that even all truth out of any truth may be concluded,) howbeit no man bound in such sort to deduce all his actions out of Scripture, as if either the place be to him unknown whereon they may be concluded, or the reference unto that place not presently considered of, the action shall in that respect be condemned as unlawful.[19]

---

[17] 120, I, 238.   [18] 120, I, 239–40.   [19] 57, I, 288: *Laws*, II, i, 2.

Hooker often seems to suggest that his adversaries call for a precise legalism of this sort, and that they do not really believe in the pervasive harmony of nature and scripture upon which he bases his reply to them, but he nowhere actually says so.[20] Instead, he argues in the manner of one seeking to coax together in some rather poorly instructed minds certain beliefs which must surely be there, but in a scattered state. The only error he really attributes to them is a failure to appreciate the full implications of the principle that nature accords with scripture. Such undoubtedly is Hooker's sincere impression of the state of the Puritan mind, and the polemic strategy based on it proved its worth in the event. The Puritans found Hooker unanswerable precisely because he caused the whole debate to centre on a principle of which they had never had any doubt, the harmony between natural and revealed truth. He was able to do so because of the fundamental difficulty that Whitgift had revealed in the Puritan conception of scriptural authority, simply by challenging Cartwright to say what the difference was between ordering indifferent matters in a manner 'not repugnant to' the general precepts of scripture and ordering them 'according to' scripture.

Attempting to answer the challenge, Cartwright in effect recognizes the difficulty. He begins by tracing the debate on the meaning of scriptural authority to the point of impasse:

The Admonition said that nothing ought to be established in the church which is not commanded by the word of God: the A[nswerer] offended herewith condemned this saying: the reply sheweth how the saying of the A[dmonition] is maintainable, namely for that though there be not express words for every thing which may be established, yet there are general commandments whereby all things which can fall into any ecclesiastical consultation are to be directed. The A[nswerer] ... saith: that in those things which are varied by time and other circumstances and whereof there is no precise determination in the word of God, it is enough that they be not against the word of God. So that this is the difference between the Adm[onition] and him: they will have those things not only to be against the word but to be grounded upon the word, and he saith it is enough they be not against the word. Wherein if there were no diversity the Ans[werer] is in fault, which in his greediness of finding fault condemneth that in the Adm[onition] which he is constrained to allow of.

[20] See note 12 above.

With at least equal justice he may himself be said to condemn in his adversary that which he is 'constrained to allow of' himself. Nevertheless, even while conceding the logical equivalence of the two ways of expressing agreement with scripture, he continues to insist:

But indeed they are not all one. For albeit it cannot be but that which is not agreeable unto the word of God is against the word of God, and of the other side that which is not against the word of God is agreeable unto it; yet he that so saith that certain things must be done not against the word, that he will not also accord that they should be done according to the word, giveth thereby to understand that there is some star or light of reason or learning or other help whereby some act may be well done, and acceptably unto God, in which the word of God was shut out and not called to counsel, as that which either could not or need not give any direction in that behalf.[21]

Hooker will call this 'the last refuge in maintaining [the Puritan] position':

... that is to say, all Church orders must be 'grounded upon the word of God;' in such sort grounded upon the word, not that being found out by some 'star, or light of reason, or learning, or other help,' they may be received, so they be not against the word of God; but according at leastwise unto the general rules of Scripture they must be made. Which is in effect as much as to say, 'We know not what to say well in defence of this position; and therefore lest we should say it is false, there is no remedy but to say that in some sense or other it may be true, if we could tell how.'[22]

Hooker's triumph is logically well founded. Cartwright has made a carefully explicit acknowledgment of the basic principle upon which the claim of the Anglican Church to scriptural authority rests, that positive and negative formulations of the meaning of obedience to God's word are logically equivalent; yet he persists in requiring a positive statement. Hooker understandably takes him to be trying to bluster his way out of a logical trap of his own devising, and does not refrain from enjoying the spectacle.

Yet in his very confession of logical discomfiture the Puritan achieves his clearest demonstration of the difference between his attitude toward scripture and the Conformist's. It cannot be explained in logical or epistemological terms; it is a difference,

[21] 17, 55-6.
[22] 57, I, 364: *Laws*, III, viii, 1.

rather, in the way in which the mind is conscious of being affected in its operations by the Bible. Logically it makes no difference whether a proposition be said to agree or merely not to disagree with general principles found in scripture; all the same it makes all the difference in the world in which sense an act is conceived to be directed by the word of God. The double negative, 'not against' or 'not repugnant to', expresses an indirect and incidental kind of agreement with scripture which the Puritan, though he cannot deny its logical sufficiency, finds wanting. For the Puritan an act may be 'according to' the word of God in the logical sense in which 'not against' the word means the same thing, and yet not constitute obedience to God; it may be 'well done' in that it corresponds to rational and consequently to scriptural principles, and yet not 'well done, and acceptably unto God' if 'the word of God was shut out and not called to counsel, as that which either could not or need not give any direction in that behalf'.

Thus the two parties approach the question of the relationship between reason and scripture with the same logical and epistemological assumptions but with different preoccupations. For the Puritan, obedience to God's word must be something more than a rational adjustment of man's behaviour to God's truth, although undoubtedly it is that. He insists on trying to hear God's voice of command in all his thoughts and cannot feel that he is obeying God if it is 'shut out'. Directions simply found out by reason, reliable or not, can no more be equivalent to scriptural direction for him than a good map of the country could have done duty for the pillar of cloud that went before the people of God in Exodus; 'it is necessary', Cartwright says, 'to have the word of God go before us in all our actions ... for that we cannot otherwise be assured that they please God.'[23] The Conformist, on the other hand, in following the dictates of reason alone is conscious of obeying some part of God's law in much the same way as he is when acting in accordance with any other part of the harmonious structure of universal truth. The truth he is acting upon in the one case is, to be sure, of a higher order than in the other, but obedience in either case consists in conforming action to knowledge. When he does not find direction 'in manifest words contained in scripture, or thereof gathered by necessary collection', he can indeed rest assured that scripture 'need not give any direction in that behalf'. In proceeding

[23] 17, 61.

thereupon to let reason be his guide, he does not feel any such loss of the sense of obedience to God as the Puritan would feel. Conversely, he sees nothing to be gained by insisting that things not distinctly expressed in the words of the Bible are 'commanded' in some sense by the word of God.

This confidence that natural reason, where applicable, is equivalent to scriptural law is itself indisputably scriptural, as Hooker points out, and specifically Pauline:

Doth not the Apostle term the law of nature [Rom. 1:32], even as the evangelist doth the law of Scripture [Luke 1:6], δικαίωμα τοῦ θεοῦ God's own righteous ordinance? The law of nature then being his law, that must needs be of him which it hath directed men unto. Great odds I grant there is between things devised by men, although agreeable with the law of nature, and things in Scripture set down by the finger of the Holy Ghost. Howbeit the dignity of these is no hindrance, but that those be also reverently accounted of in their place.[24]

The Epistle to the Romans, and thus the canonical exposition of Pauline theology itself, opens with an account of the relation between the law which God has revealed to his chosen people and the laws which the mind of Greece has discovered in the universal nature of things. Paul says as distinctly as the Elizabethan Conformist could wish that the two kinds of law are to a very large extent equivalent.

Paul takes up this subject in the first place in order to explain how people 'without the law' can enter into equal fellowship in Christ with the people of the Book. The problem of the Apostle to the Gentiles is to explain how this can be without derogating God's historical revelation of his will to his chosen people. The solution Paul offers is made possible by the central paradox of his thought concerning the law. The law serves, not to justify, but to make men aware of their absolute inability to achieve justification, thus preparing them to receive the grace of God in Christ. It does so by presenting an image of perfection against which man's works are to be measured and inevitably found wanting, and for this sad purpose the moral law which all men can learn by examining themselves and the nature of God's creation can suffice. Thus, as Hooker says,

Under the name of the Law, we must comprehend not only that which God hath written in tables and leaves, but that which nature hath en-

[24] 57, III, 213: *Laws*, VII, xi, 10.

graved in the hearts of men. Else how should those heathen, which never had books but heaven and earth to look upon, be convicted of perverseness? 'But the Gentiles, which had not the law in books, had,' saith the Apostle, 'the effect of the law written in their hearts' [Rom. 2:14–15].[25]

Reason, like the law, leaves man 'without excuse' (1:20).

Since Paul is mainly concerned to show that man's natural reason will do to be damned by, his defence of it at this point can hardly be described as a manifesto of humanism. However, he also wishes to combat self-righteousness among the Jewish possessors of the law, and to remind them that mere knowledge of the law counts for nothing—'For not the hearers of the law are just before God, but the doers of the law shall be justified' (2:13)—and so his central thesis concerning the use of natural morality is complicated by a polemical comparison between Jews who, having the law, neglect it in practice, and Gentiles who 'have not the law', yet 'do by nature the things contained in the law' (2:14). Thus a more appreciative note comes into his description of those who, 'having not the law, are a law unto themselves: Which shew the work of the law written in their hearts, their conscience also bearing witness' (2:14–15), and by reading Paul's phrases in the light of the Fourth Gospel, Hooker can find in them the very foundation of Christian humanism:

The light of natural understanding, wit, and reason, is from God; he it is which thereby doth illuminate every man entering into the world [John 1:9]. If there proceed from us any thing afterwards corrupt and naught, the mother thereof is our own darkness, neither doth it proceed from any such cause whereof God is the author. He is the author of all that we think or do by virtue of that light, which himself hath given. And therefore the laws which the very heathens did gather to direct their actions by, so far forth as they proceeded from the light of nature, God himself doth acknowledge [Rom. 2:19; 2:15] to have proceeded even from himself, and that he was the writer of them in the tables of their hearts.[26]

---

[25] 57, III, 600: Sermon III, 1.

[26] 57, I, 383: *Laws*, III, ix, 3. The Authorized Version (like Tyndale's and the Vulgate) resolves the syntactical ambiguity of John 1:9, Ἦν τὸ φῶς τὸ ἀληθινὸν ὃ φωτίζει πάντα ἄνθρωπον ἐρχόμενον εἰς τὸν κόσμον, by taking ἐρχόμενον with πάντα ἄνθρωπον. The context favours the alternative which appears in most modern versions: '(6) There was sent by God a man named John (7) who came as a witness to testify to the light so that through him all men might believe—(8) but only to testify to the light, for he himself was not the light. (9)

The law, though sinful man must come to apprehend it as a condemnation and a curse, is itself 'holy, and the commandment holy,
just, and good', Paul proclaims (7:12); and so, the Christian
humanist can be sure, is the natural order.

Whoever believes in Christ is freed from the condemnation of
the law: Paul calls the Psalmist to witness, 'Blessed is the man to
whom the Lord will not impute sin' (4:8), which becomes in
Christian humanist paraphrase, 'Beatus vir, cui non imputarit
Dominus peccatum. Audis remitti iniquitates, adversus legem
Mosaicam commissas. Audis obtegi peccata, adversus naturae
legem patrata.'[27] Similarly the law of nature can be understood
alternatively to the Mosaic law in the arguments by which Paul
explains that his new freedom from the curse of the law does not
license us henceforth to sin against it. Far from voiding nature and
civilization of religious value, Pauline Christianity can be said to
'establish' both, just as Paul says 'we establish the law' (3:31).
Such are the demonstrable implications which the Anglican Conformist appreciates fully in the Epistle to the Romans, perhaps more
fully than the Puritan, who, however, at least cannot deny them.

Nevertheless, the Puritan's discontent with this manner of inte-
grating scripture with nature may serve to bring out a difficulty
latent in the argument of the Epistle to the Romans. When the
positive implications of Paul's treatment of the law of nature are
expanded upon, the special place reserved in the scheme of things
for the law of Moses comes to seem merely honorary, so to speak.
Indeed, where scripture and nature teach the same laws, it may
even seem that the greater reverence should be paid to nature as
the primary text, upon which scripture is, at those points, only a
helpful commentary. Hooker feels called upon to explain why it is
not 'vain that the Scripture aboundeth with so great store of laws
in this kind', which he does by pointing out that

... they are either such as we of ourselves could not easily have found
out, and then the benefit is not small to have them readily set down to

The real light which gives light to every man was coming into the world!'
(trans. Raymond E. Brown, *The Anchor Bible* (12)). Here the emphasis is
evenly distributed between the assertion that the light is eternal and universal
and the assertion that it came into the world at a particular historical moment.
Thus, while this place can still support Hooker's identification of the light with
'natural understanding, wit, and reason', it does so less simply and emphatically than the version he uses.

[27] 38, 30: ad loc.

our hands; or if they be so clear and manifest that no man endued with reason can lightly be ignorant of them, yet the Spirit as it were borrowing them from the school of Nature, as serving to prove things less manifest, and to induce a persuasion of somewhat which were in itself more hard and dark, unless it should in such sort be cleared, the very applying of them unto cases particular is not without most singular use and profit many ways for men's instruction. Besides, be they plain of themselves or obscure, the evidence of God's own testimony added to the natural assent of reason concerning the certainty of them, doth not a little comfort and confirm the same.[28]

But with all due regard to the comfort and confirmation which scripture can bring to the deliberations of men, 'the unseparable law of nature'[29] does quite well without it. 'If God had never spoken word unto men concerning the duty which children owe unto their parents, yet from the firstborn of Adam unto the last of us, "Honor thy father and thy mother," could not but have tied all.'[30] It begins to seem as though Paul's argument did in fact 'make void' the scriptural form of moral law, not by giving men licence to act otherwise than it would prescribe, but in another, subtler sense, one which Paul himself—'Hebrew of the Hebrews' —might have found as unacceptable as did the English Puritans.

In the Epistle to the Romans Paul pursues an unsolved problem to an *o altitudo*: the reconciliation in Christ of Jew with Greek. He points toward an ultimate concord between two antithetical ways of conceiving human identity and obligation. Hebrew thought conceives of a unique expression of the will of God, delivered to God's chosen people, written, as it were, by the moving finger of God in that people's history; Greek thought seeks that which is not unique and historical but universal and timeless. Although the Greek readily conceives of law as derived from God, he must conceive of it as addressed to no one particularly but as indifferently patent to the investigations of all. His basic concept of obligation does not support the identity of a people or a person, except in the sense that the mind may congratulate itself on becoming conscious of the necessities under which it exists. One way to apprehend the meaning of the Gospel as Paul teaches it is to see in it a mysterious reconciliation between the universalism of Greek rationality and the precious particularism of the Jewish tradition.

[28] 57, I, 262: *Laws*, I, xii, 1.
[29] 57, III, 285: *Laws*, VII, xxii, 5.
[30] 57, III, 619: Sermon III, 2.

The concentration of post-exilic Judaism on the written form of the law may be seen to express in a somewhat novel and, so to speak, 'stylized' fashion Israel's original sense of obedience to God's commands. The very idea of the sacred written record expresses the essential characteristic of uniqueness in Israel's relation to God, its inseparableness from a particular history. This conception is, to employ the suggestive term coined by Wilhelm Windelband, 'idiographic'. Windelband used the term to describe the kind of understanding sought characteristically in the study of history, which tries to realize the full, unrecurrent particularity of events and of relationships among events, whereas the natural sciences, which Windelband characterized as 'nomothetic', seek general laws.[31] Whatever value these terms may have in the uses they have been put to by Windelband himself and others,[32] they

[31] 'So dürfen wir sagen: die Erfahrungswissenschaften suchen in der Erkenntnis des Wirklichen entweder das Allgemeine in der Form des Naturgesetzes oder das Einzelne in der geschichtlich bestimmten Gestalt; sie betrachten zu einem Teil die immer sich gleichbleibende Form, zum anderen Teil den einmaligen, in sich bestimmten Inhalt des wirklichen Geschehens. Die einen sind Gesetzeswissenschaften, die anderen Ereigniswissenschaften; jene lehren, was immer ist, diese, was einmal war. Das wissenschaftliche Denken ist—wenn man neue Kunstausdrücke bilden darf—in dem einen Falle nomothetisch, in dem andern idiographisch. Wollen wir uns an die gewohnten Ausdrücke halten, so dürfen wir ferner in diesem Sinne von dem Gegensatz naturwissenschaftlicher und historischer Disciplinen reden, vorausgesetzt dass wir in Errinerung behalten, in diesem methodischen Sinne die Psychologie durchaus zu den Naturwissenschaften zu zählen' (121, 12).

[32] Erwin Panofsky applies Windelband's terms in a suggestive analogy with the fine arts: 'Classical art corresponds to the natural "sciences", which see abstract (viz., quantitative) and universal laws realized in an individual case (for example, the law of gravity in the falling apple); Northern art corresponds to the humanistic, that is to say, historical, disciplines which view the individual case as a link in a greater, but still concrete (viz., qualitative) and, within its wider scope, still individual "sequence" (for example, the changes in the statutes of a particular guild as an instance of the "process of development" from the Middle Ages to modern times). Where the natural scientist proceeds idiographically (e.g., when a geographer describes a particular mountain), he may be said to consider this mountain not as a part of nature in general but as a phenomenon *sui iuris*, as something that has evolved, and not as something that has been caused. Conversely, where the humanist proceeds nomothetically (e.g., when a student of economic history attempts to establish certain laws for which universal validity is claimed), he may be said to operate as a would-be scientist' (*Meaning in the Visual Arts* (Garden City, New York: Doubleday Anchor Books [unsewn], 1955), p. 270 n.). Panofsky's identification of 'idiographic' with 'humanistic' seems especially curious in view of the analogy which he is suggesting between nomothetic sciences and classical Greek art, from which he surely does not mean to suggest withdrawing the epithet 'humanistic'. None the less, the impulse to identify idiographic with humanistic does testify to the

seem especially apt for describing the difference between Hebrew and Greek ways of seeking religious significance in human experience.

An idiographic conception of things arranges them in a unique continuum and sees the significance of any item or event as consisting in the relationships between it and all the others in that continuum. A person's memory of the time he has lived, together with his sense of expectation and apprehension, forms such a continuum or developing complex; the history of a people can come to form another; and when a devout Pharisee like the young Paul of Tarsus seeks the law of his life in scripture, he is referring his present moment of life to the memory of God's dealings with Israel. The nomothetic Greek mind, on the other hand, seeks laws which can be abstracted from any particular set of things, and sees the significance of any item or event as consisting in the general principles which it exhibits. The two approaches seem mutually exclusive, each claiming to provide the true explanation of the other. On the one hand, the history of biblical thought—from Moses' recasting of Egyptian lore, through the long ages of interaction between Yahwism and the cyclical fertility cults of Canaan, down to Paul's transformation of whatever suggestions he took from the mysteries or from Greek philosophy—can be described as the successive enrichment of an idiographic tradition by taking into itself, and thus radically changing, nomothetic forms and conceptions. On the other hand, once a nomothetic account of a given item or event or history has been given, that account by its very nature claims to subsume any idiographic one. That is, once the set of relationships which constitute the idiographic significance of a given item or event comes to be seen as an instance of a general law, the uniqueness of that set of relationships is *eo ipso* lost. Once the Jewish tradition is seen as an expression of the morality implicit in the nature of things generally, it is difficult to retain a sense of the unique value of that tradition.

In the Epistle to the Romans this antimony does not make itself felt immediately; the difficulty can emerge, as has been seen, only when the implications of Paul's treatment of natural law are pursued beyond the point of defining its function in leading men to

impersonality of nomothetic conceptions and to the sense that an idiographic way of thinking about human events preserves a special element of humanity in them.

Christ. It is only when the pertinence of natural law to life 'in Christ' comes to be discussed that there may be occasion for the kind of dissatisfaction that the Puritan feels. It is then that the kind of response to God's will which the old attitude toward scripture represents may seem to be eliminated from Christian life, the moral parts of the Old Law being simply assimilated into the general world of Greek thought. But when Paul speaks of the relation of moral law to the 'newness of life' of those who have been 'baptized into Jesus Christ' (6:3–4), it is always the Jewish Law that he has in mind, never the law of nature. Furthermore, when he says that 'the righteousness of the Law [is] fulfilled in us, who walk not after the flesh but after the spirit' (8:4) he cannot mean simply that those who are 'in Christ' henceforth conform unerringly to the moral precepts of the Old Law, which would amount to the same thing as conforming to those of natural law. He necessarily means something both less than that and more: less, because he everywhere shows, most obviously by the urgency of his exhortations to his 'children in Christ', that he does not suppose they are faultless in fact; and more, because the fulfillment of the Law is not to be understood apart from the fulfillment of God's promise to his people. It is the scriptural kind of obedience that is to be fulfilled by 'bringing every thought into captivity to the obedience of Christ' (2 Cor. 10:5).

This imperative could hardly be felt by minds wholly Greek. Once the Pauline mission of bringing together Jew and Greek to form the new people of God in Christ had failed historically, leaving the Greek mind in sole possession of the new religion, Paul's formulations could only be understood as bearing on the characteristically Greek preoccupation with abstract knowledge.[33] They would inevitably be scanned for implications concerning the relationship between rational or empirical knowledge and revealed truth, philosophy and theology, science and religion. Thus where Paul says, in Romans 1:19, that the Gentiles can find out from nature sufficient knowledge of God to leave them 'without excuse', Origen's Commentary brings out the thought that truth about God is divided into two kinds:

[33] For classic discussions of the Hellenizing of Christianity see Edwin Hatch, *The Influence of Greek Ideas on Christianity* (52), especially Chapters 11 and 12, and Adolph Harnack, *History of Dogma* (51), especially the first two of the seven volumes.

Because that which may be known of God is manifest in them; for God hath shewed it unto them. We have already said above, that what may be known of God is that which they [natural men] can find out from the order of consequences in this world or from rational theories, as the Apostle himself also points out in saying that the invisible things of God are seen through those things that are made. What cannot be known of God, however, is to be understood to be the mode of his substance or nature; what his properties are is hidden, I think, not only from us men but from all creatures. Or rather, it is for God alone to know whether sometimes there will be such an improvement in rational nature that it may come to that knowledge also. It seems to me that some such thing is to be hoped for from these things that are said by our Saviour: *that no man knoweth the Son, but the Father; neither knoweth any man the Father, save the Son, and to whomsoever the Son will reveal him.* For he would not have added, *and to whomsoever the Son will reveal him,* unless he knew there were some to whom he would reveal him.[34]

Since scripture itself is recorded revelation, it is welcomed as the final resource of philosophy, as in Justin's *Dialogue with Trypho*:

'Whom else then, I reply, could one take as teacher, or from what quarter might one derive advantage, if the truth is not even in these philosophers?'

'There were a long time ago men of greater antiquity than all these reputed philosophers, men blessed and righteous and beloved of God who spake by the Divine Spirit, and foretold those things of the future, which indeed have come to pass. Prophets do men call them. They, and they only, saw the truth and declared it to mankind, without fear or shame of any, not dominated by ambition, but saying only what they had heard and seen, filled as they were with the Holy Spirit.

'Now their writings still remain with us even to the present time, and it is open to anyone to consult these, and to gain most valuable knowledge both about the origin of things and their end, and all else that a philosopher ought to know, if he believes what they say. For they have not made their discourses, when they wrote, with logical proof, inasmuch as being trustworthy witnesses of the truth they are superior to all such proof, but the things that did take place and are taking place now compel agreement with what they have spoken.'[35]

Thus while philosophy is subordinated to scripture as an ultimate authority, scripture is made to serve the purposes of philosophy.

[34] Translated from the condensed Latin version of Rufinus (82, 865).
[35] 60, 14–15: Ch. VII, 1–2.

The question of the relationship between the general law of nature and the Jewish scriptural tradition comes to be understood as a philosophical question of the relationship between reason and revelation as means of arriving at knowledge.

This is the conception of the use of scripture to which Hooker appeals in answer to what he takes to be the perverse insistence of the Puritans that 'The word of God containeth whatsoever things can fall into any part of man's life':

Whatsoever either men on earth or the Angels of heaven do know, it is as a drop of that unemptiable fountain of wisdom; which wisdom hath diversely imparted her treasures unto the world. As her ways are of sundry kinds, so her manner of teaching is not merely one and the same. Some things she openeth by the sacred books of Scripture; some things by the glorious works of Nature: with some things she inspireth them from above by spiritual influence; in some things she leadeth and traineth them only by worldly experience and practice. We may not so in any one special kind admire her, that we disgrace her in any other; but let all her ways be according unto their place and degree adored.[36]

Those things which eternal wisdom 'openeth by the sacred books of Scripture' are to be sought there by appropriate methods of investigation, just as are those things which are imparted by other kinds of evidence. The authority of scripture is that of an infallible document from which the most important of all knowledge is to be sought, but in a manner no different from 'the principles of all kinds of knowledge else' that books may contain:

The end of the word of God is *to save*, and therefore we term it *the word of life*. The way for all men to be saved is by the knowledge of that truth which the word hath taught. . . . To this end the word of God no otherwise serveth than only in the nature of a doctrinal instrument. It saveth because it maketh 'wise to salvation' [2 Tim. 3 : 15]. . . . And concerning our Assent to the mysteries of heavenly truth, seeing that the word of God for the Author's sake hath credit with all that confess it (as we all do) to be his word, every proposition of holy Scripture, every sentence being to us a principle; if the principles of all kinds of knowledge else have that virtue in themselves, whereby they are able to procure our assent unto such conclusions as the industry of right discourse doth gather from them; we have no reason to think the principles of that truth which tendeth unto man's everlasting happiness less forcible than

[36] 57, I, 290: *Laws*, II, i, 4.

any other, when we know that of all other they are for their certainty the most infallible.[37]

What is being described here is not the Conformist's total appreciation of the Bible, of course, but his conception of the sense in which its authority is to be appealed to. As a 'doctrinal instrument' it supplies authoritative axioms from which saving knowledge is to be deduced by 'the industry of right discourse'.

In protesting that this conception of the manner in which thought and action are to be directed by scripture is 'not enough', Puritanism revives the antinomy between two ways of thought which Paul had seen resolved in Christ, but which had been dissolved, rather, in post-Pauline, Hellenistic Christianity. The Puritan senses strongly the import of the scriptural concept of obligation, and in his conviction that a special sense of response to God's special will is not 'shut out' by the new dispensation he grasps a vital and elusive element in Pauline theology. In all his insistence on that element, however, he by no means renounces the thought-world of Greece. The questions concerning the means of knowing truth to which Whitgift and Hooker naturally assume the debate is addressed do not really trouble the Puritan, whose very commitment to formal disputation—his readiness to argue about the distribution of terms in a syllogism, for instance—expresses unquestioning acceptance of the system of knowledge set forth by Hooker. Therein lies the root of the peculiar difficulty that becomes apparent in these frustrating intellectual encounters between Puritans and Conformists. The syntax and vocabulary of thought in which the discussion is cast accommodate one element of the Puritan concept of scriptural authority so completely as to leave the other—that which distinguishes the Puritan from his opponent—almost unexpressible. The apparatus of logical demonstration, developed out of the Greek interest in discovering abstract truth, itself implies that preoccupation and tends to transform all others into it. The Puritan is trying in effect to make that system of discourse convey motives of thought other than those which, by its very nature, it presupposes, while still remaining faithful to its own.

If this radical difficulty accounts for the weakness of the Puritan's position on the meaning of scriptural authority, the

[37] 57, II, 85–6: *Laws*, xxi, 3.

Conformist's obliviousness to the difficulty is the strength of his. His rationalism is not complicated by motives of thought other than those congenial to it. Because he does not sense any need to combine the conception of scripture as a source of authoritative 'principles' with any other conception of scriptural authority, the difficulty of doing so tends in itself to confirm his position. Hooker can answer Puritanism by a comprehensive assertion of the power of the Greek thought-world to assimilate the Bible. Yet the Puritan insists that his requirements of Church polity are quite rational and general, thus variable in practice according to circumstances—not tied to a precise interpretation of specific texts—, and at the same time that they answer a uniquely biblical imperative to the exclusion of any other polity. When asked in general terms how this can be, he hardly fares better than Hooker says: 'in some sense or other it may be true, if we could tell how.'

II

CHRISTIAN LIBERTY AND EDIFICATION

THE first challenge to the Elizabethan Church settlement from the Protestant side was made in the name of Christian liberty. For the English Church to require its ministers to wear the surplice and perform certain of the ceremonies of the Roman Church seemed to some a reversion to the bondage from which Christ freed mankind:

Now, these garments which in popery have belonged to Idols, are filthy Idolothytes, that served unto Devils. Therefore are they against Christian liberty. Again, to bind men to eat Idolothytes, were against Christian liberty: therefore to bind men to wear the Idolothytes, is against Christian liberty. To command them to wear Garlands, Palms, Hats, or earrings, like the Idolaters, were against Christian liberty. Therefore to bind them to cover all their bodies with Idolatrous garments, is against Christian liberty. To bind men to observe Jewish Ceremonies, were against Christian liberty. Therefore are such commandments, in the ceremonies, of Antichrist, against Christian liberty.[1]

To the Bishops the case seemed just the opposite. Christian liberty meant precisely that they were free to use 'extern things' as they chose; those people who objected to the use of certain vestments in the Church were the real enemies of Christian liberty. Matthew Parker writes:

It is not unknown what arguments and conclusions, what letters and writings have been used and tossed from man to man in secret sort, for these two or three years, to disprove the liberty of the children of God in the use of extern things, to convel [i.e., disturb] the obedience that true Subjects should perform to the authority of their Prince, & to the laws of the Realm established, to the discrediting and condemnation of such which in a whole conscience think it lawful for them to wear, and yet charitably bearing with the weakness of such whose consciences are entangled with fearful scrupulosity toward the same.[2]

---

[1] 48, Sig. K7 and verso.
[2] 83, unmarked first page.

The Puritans' insistence that 'whatsoever is not done by the word of God is sin' seems to Whitgift to 'bring a great servitude and bondage to the conscience, restrain or rather utterly overthrow that part of Christian liberty which consisteth in the free use of indifferent things, neither commanded nor forbidden in the word of God, and throw men headlong into desperation'.[3] Cartwright answers that 'the fault is in his want of understanding. For even those things that are indifferent and may be done have their freedom grounded of the word of God....'[4] Thus the two parties respond in opposite ways to Paul's admonition to 'Stand fast ... in the liberty wherewith Christ hath made us free, and be not entangled again with the yoke of bondage' (Gal. 5:1).

Nevertheless, in the accounts they give of Christian liberty in terms of legal theory the two parties agree. Both accept the usual distinctions between the ceremonial, judicial, and moral parts of the Old Law. The ceremonial ordinances are no longer binding in any way, their legal force having passed into typological significance. They were veiled expressions of truth that has been revealed clearly in Christ, so that to obey them literally would be a retreat into the old darkness. The judicial parts of the Old Law remain in force only to the extent that the circumstances they dealt with remain the same, which is often not the case. Cartwright explains:

And, as for the judicial law, forasmuch as there are some of them made in regard of the region where they were given, and of the people to whom they were given, the prince and magistrate, keeping the substance and equity of them (as it were the marrow), may change the circumstances of them, as the times and places and manners of the people shall require.[5]

The moral law, however, 'is in as full strength as ever it was before the coming of our Saviour Christ'.[6] The Christian is freed from it,

[3] 120, I, 194.

[4] 17, 59.

[5] 120, I, 270. Cartwright differs from Whitgift (and, as Whitgift points out, from Calvin also) in arguing that, by this principle, the Deuteronomical death penalty for idolaters should still be in force, the relevant circumstances not having changed in the least (120, I, 270 ff. and 17, 96–7). The principle from which he argues to this appalling conclusion is Whitgift's also, though the Conformist's logical consistency suffers in this instance for the sake of political prudence (120, I, 270 ff.) and humane forbearance (120, I, 329 ff.).

[6] 17, 96. Cf. Hooker: 'Christ, in works ceremonial, giveth more liberty, in moral much less, than they [the Scribes and Pharisees] did.' 57, III, 529: Sermon II, 30.

not in the sense of its having become irrelevant to him, but because it no longer condemns him—he is justified in Christ—and, to the extent that 'sanctification' has proceeded in him, he no longer feels the moral law as an alien constraint. Puritans and Conformists both assume these principles. In doctrinal terms no difference appears between them concerning Christian liberty.

For the Conformist, this very fact—that the doctrine of the Church of England with respect to Christian liberty is unexceptionable—suffices to establish the liberty of a Christian man in England. Just as the Conformist defines the authority of the Bible as that of a 'doctrinal instrument', so he refers Christian liberty entirely to knowledge in the strict sense of doctrinal instruction. So long as doctrine is kept pure, Christian liberty is assured, since whatever gestures he may perform, or whatever garments he may put on, the well-instructed Christian is free to think nothing of them. His liberty consists in his knowledge that such things have no religious significance in themselves but are only to be complied with out of respect for conventional decency. Since conventions are by their nature arbitrary, the secular authorities can legitimately decide what is 'decent': 'If you will yet doubt of comeliness and decency, then I still say unto you that what is comely and decent is not every man's part to judge, but the magistrate's, and such as have authority in the church.'[7] If what the civil authorities decide is to impose ceremonies and vestments which bear the appearance of religious efficacy in themselves, having long been used with superstitious reverence, the remedy is simply to instruct the people better in the doctrine of Christian liberty: 'If in case any of the people be persuaded that these things savour of papism, monachism, or Judaism, let them be told the contrary, and perfectly instructed therein.'[8] As the Conformist understands it, Christian

---

[7] 120, II, 58.

[8] 120, II, 41 (quoting a letter from Bullinger to Sampson and Humphrey, 1566). Bucer's advice to the puzzled English was the same: 'They that be such Ministers of the Churches of England may, as I think, wear with God's pleasure, those vestures which be at this day in use: And they I think shall do so much the better after they have preached the clear doctrine of Christ our Saviour, with the detection and detestation, as well of the whole Antichrist of Rome, as of any other adversary to Christ: If they then profess, by the wearing of these garments, to have no purpose at all to stablish any wicked devices that Antichrist hath obtruded to the people: Nor that Priests be of themselves more holy, or more able to pacify God, than other Christian men be ...' ('The aunswere of M. Bucer to the foresayde letters', appended to *A briefe examination*, (83) Sig. A2ᵛ). For

liberty derives from the autonomy of doctrine. It can be summed up by the adage 'Thought is free.'

This conception reflects the well-known Elizabethan policy of not meddling with the subject's thoughts provided he conform outwardly to established institutions. Christian liberty becomes, in fact, the basic principle of Elizabethan Erastianism, since it amounts to saying that matters which were once prescribed as religious duties by the word of God can now be regulated for civil purposes by the magistrate. In contrast, the Puritan's idea of Christian liberty is precisely what causes him to resist Elizabeth's policy:

> And if the Prince shall take in hand to command us to do any of those things which God hath not commanded, in such sort that we may not leave them undone unless we will thereby run into the penalty of the law (when we shall see that in doing thereof we cannot edify but destroy) we must then refuse to do the thing commanded by the Prince, and humbly submit ourselves to suffer the penalty, but in any case not content to infringe the Christian liberty, which is to use things indifferent, to edification and not to destruction.[9]

The Puritan thinks of Christian liberty less as a permission than as a command. To do 'any of those things which God hath not commanded' would be, not an assertion, but a violation of Christian liberty. Far from consigning authority in 'extern things' entirely

a full account of Bucer's correspondence on this question see Constantin Hopf, *Martin Bucer and the English Reformation* (58, 131–70). This solution served its turn in the early days of the Elizabethan settlement, but Hooker sees as clearly as any radical Puritan that the version of the 'middle way' which it represents is really an excluded middle. The mock-sermon which he composes to be delivered 'in pensive manner' by a disgruntled wearer of the surplice would bear as scathingly on the first generation of Anglican bishops, including Jewel, as on the relatively conservative Puritans who are Hooker's contemporary opponents, but Hooker deflects it onto Bullinger and Bucer: 'Those good and learned men which gave the first direction to this course had reason to wish that their own proceedings at home might be favoured abroad also, and that the good affection of such as inclined towards them might be kept alive. But if themselves had gone under those sails which they require to be hoisted up, if they had been themselves to execute their own theory in this church, I doubt not but easily they would have seen being nearer at hand, that the way was not good which they took of advising men . . . they would easily have seen how with us it cannot be endured to hear a man openly profess that he putteth fire to his neighbour's house, but yet so halloweth the same with prayer that he hopeth it shall not burn' (57, II, 137–8: *Laws*, V, xxix, 8).

[9] 31, Sig. Bii^v–Biii.

to the magistrate, Christian liberty engages the subject to civil disobedience on occasion in order to 'use things indifferent, to edification and not to destruction'.

This phrase, which to the modern reader is likely to seem merely a vague platitude, provides the key to the Puritan's understanding of Christian liberty, and in fact to the whole mystery of Elizabethan Puritanism.[10] It is not too much to say that the whole, subtle but radical difference between the Puritan cast of mind and the Conformist appears in their different ways of understanding the verb 'to edify'.

Saint Paul uses the verb οἰκοδομέω, 'to build a house' or 'to build', and the noun formed from it, οἰκοδομή, 'building', in a way for which there is no exact precedent, and which the Latinate-English 'to edify' and 'edification' only partially preserve, even though Paul's usage evidently accounts for the currency of these words taken in a figurative sense exclusively.[11] Paul's usage of οἰκοδομέω derives from the Septuagint rendering of the Hebrew *banah* (and the Aramaic *bena'*). This theme of 'building a house' develops important meaning in the Old Testament, and Paul can be seen to resume that development in his use of οἰκοδομέω, combining the already heavily freighted Hebrew motif with a characteristically Hellenic commonplace, so that his usage of the word οἰκοδομέω and its compounds provides an instructive epitome of the interaction of Jewish and Hellenic conceptions in his thought. It concerns particularly the relation between individual and communal religious life, as Elizabethan Puritans recognized.

The Old Testament conceives of communal identity entirely in terms of the patriarchal family or 'house'.[12] Procreation,

[10] Crowley (see foregoing note) 'expounds the thesis that ministers should "edifie or build up the Church of Christ," as authority for which he cites four chapters from the Epistles of St. Paul, which were to become basic in Puritan dialectic, namely, II Corinthians xiii., Ephesians ii. and iv., and I Corinthians xiv., in each of which St. Paul refers to the church as the house of God to be "edified," or built by its members. From this time on, the most inclusive of these texts, St. Paul's exhortation, I Corinthians xiv. 26., "Let all things be done unto edifying," becomes the battle-cry of the "hot gospeller"' (Donald Joseph McGinn, *The Admonition Controversy* (66, 17–18)).

[11] See entries in Liddell and Scott, and in Kittel, *Theologisches Wörterbuch zum Neuen Testament*. The present discussion relies particularly on Philipp Vielhauer, Oikodome: *Das Bild vom Bau* . . . (115). See also Joseph Pfammatter, *Die Kirche Als Bau* . . . (90).

[12] 'Prehistoric Israel is to us a closed book; but whatever may be true of that epoch, there is no doubt that from the time of our oldest documents, at any rate,

considered as the strengthening and maintaining of the patriarchal family, is the 'building' of the patriarchal house. Thus barren Sarai proposes that Abram go in unto her maidservant, hoping to be 'builded' in that vicarious manner (Gen. 16:2);[13] and in the Book of Ruth, when Boaz announces his intention of marriage, the elders respond with the wish: 'The Lord make the woman that is come into thine house like Rachel and like Leah, which two did build the house of Israel' (4:11). It is appropriate to the persistent nomadic element in the traditions of Israel that this kind of 'building' should take precedence over the literal kind; the 'house' of the wandering patriarch comes before any settled habitation. The God of Israel sets his tabernacle originally not in a place but among his people, never saying to them, 'Why build ye not me an house of cedar?' (2 Sam. 7:7.)

The crisis of transition to the settled state of monarchy is marked by the delicate question of building God a house at last, a temple in Jerusalem. It is resolved for David's time in what amounts to a play on words: David is not himself to build a house for God, but God will make a 'house' for David—will establish his dynasty:

Moreover I will appoint a place for my people Israel, and will plant them, that they may dwell in a place of their own, and move no more;

the Israelite family is *patriarchal*. The proper word to describe it is *bêth 'ab*, the "house of one's father"; the genealogies are always given in the father's line, and women are rarely mentioned; and the nearest relation in the collateral line is the paternal uncle (cf. Lev. 25:49). . . .

'The family consists of those who are united by common blood and common dwelling-place. The "family" is a "house"; to found a family is "to build a house" (Neh. 7:4). . . .

'Again, the term *bêth* or "house", like the word "family" in modern languages, is very flexible and may even include the entire nation (the "house of Jacob" or the "house of Israel"), or a considerable section of the people (the "house of Joseph" or the "house of Judah") . . .' (Roland de Vaux, *Ancient Israel* (114, 20)).

The 'house' is what Johannes Pedersen describes as the 'psychic community': 'Psychic community means, above all, a common will and so a common responsibility. The man is the centre of this common will. He does not act for himself alone, but for the whole of his house. Whatever he has done, the house, the family has likewise done, for together they form an organism so closely knit that no single part thereof can be separated as something independent' (85, 271).

[13] 'The verb as it stands (Heb. *'ibbane*) can only mean "I shall be built up" (see especially xxx.3); and the usage is confirmed by Deut. xxv.9. At the same time, however, it is an obvious word play on *ben* "son", alluding to "I shall have a son", although this would not be grammatically correct' (110, 117).

... Also the Lord telleth thee that he will make thee an house (2 Sam. 7:10-11).

Under Solomon the Temple is finally built, and then, to be sure, the literal sense of 'building' comes to seem the important one for Israel. After the division of the monarchy, the policy and the religion of the Southern Kingdom are anchored to the house of David in a sense which, perforce, hardly admits distinction between the two kinds of 'building'.

Yet when the actual walls of the city and the physical edifice of the Temple come to be destroyed at last, Jeremiah can evoke anew the old sense of 'building'. It is implied, in fact, in the very words of his calling:

Then the Lord put forth his hand, and touched my mouth. And the Lord said unto me, Behold, I have put my words in thy mouth. See, I have this day set thee over the nations and over the kingdoms, to root out, and to pull down, and to destroy, and to throw down, to build, and to plant (1:9-10).

'To build and to plant' are much the same, the second member of the combined phrase being in effect epexegetic of the first, and the compound idea is set off against the idea of destruction. That compound idea emerges as a principle of policy in the letter which Jeremiah sends to the first contingent of captives in Babylon, just before the final destruction of Jerusalem and the Temple. They are not to go on resisting Babylonian rule, he tells them, but rather:

... build ye houses, and dwell in them; and plant gardens, and eat the fruit of them; take ye wives, and beget sons and daughters; and take wives for your sons, and give your daughters to husbands, that they may bear sons and daughters; that ye may be increased there, and not diminished (29:4-6).

This policy of political passivity and demotic increase is opposed directly to the militancy of the false prophets among the exiles, and more generally to all the self-reliant activity whereby the warriors and statesmen of Judah are trying to preserve the throne of David, the city, and the Temple. Destruction goes with these desperate efforts of men to preserve the structures of the kingdom, whereas true obedience to the God of Israel means fertility and growth. Jeremiah characteristically likens all human self-reliance to an effort to sustain life in a desert, whereas trust in God is like the natural adaptation of plants to a favourable environment, whereby they flourish:

Thus saith the Lord; Cursed be the man that trusteth in man, and maketh flesh his arm, and whose heart departeth from the Lord. For he shall be like the heath in the desert, and shall not see when good cometh; but shall inhabit the parched places in the wilderness, in a salt land and not inhabited. Blessed is the man that trusteth in the Lord, and whose hope the Lord is. For he shall be as a tree planted by the waters, and that spreadeth out her roots by the river, and shall not see when heat cometh, but her leaf shall be green; and shall not be careful in the year of drought, neither shall cease from yielding fruit (17:5–8).

Behind this use of the contrast between the artificial efforts of men to sustain themselves in the desert and the passive fertility of natural life can be recognized the primitivistic distrust of technological advance which is inherent in the ancient traditions of Israel. That primitivism is represented most strikingly by the neo-nomadic Rechabites of Jeremiah's own day, with whom the prophet shows marked sympathy. Jeremiah's sympathy with the Rechabites does not, however, take the literal form of abjuring houses and living in tents as they do, and he need not be supposed to disapprove literally of inventions like the cistern, whereby men are able to settle in places where there is no natural year-round water supply. Rather, he turns cultural primitivism into religious metaphor. He sees in Israel's primitivistic traditions a metaphorical expression of Israel's ancient trust in God:

Be astonished, O ye heavens, at this, and be horribly afraid, be ye very desolate, saith the Lord. For my people have committed two evils; they have forsaken me the fountain of living waters, and hewed out cisterns, broken cisterns, that can hold no water (2:12–13).

The militancy of the false prophets and the activities of the statesmen and warriors of Judah are so many efforts to patch the cisterns. To go on trusting in that kind of building will lead to the destruction of the people—in the present juncture quite literally—, whereas to trust God is 'to build and to plant' the people, even by the waters of Babylon.

With the return from the Babylonian Exile the literal sense of 'building' comes to the fore again emphatically; but some centuries thereafter the metaphorical sense—which for Israel may fairly be called the original one—is to be seen not only preserved but significantly developed in the Qumran community. In the Dead Sea texts, as Bertil Gärtner has recently shown, the rules and ideals of the Temple priests are appropriated for the Essene community:

This explains the sense in which the Dead Sea texts claim that the community constituted a new temple. Once the focus of holiness in Israel had ceased to be the temple, it was necessary to provide a new focus. This focus was the community, which called itself 'the Holy place' and 'the Holy of holies.' One of the fundamental elements in the temple symbolism of the Qumran community was a conviction that the 'presence' of God, the Spirit of God, was no longer bound to the temple in Jerusalem but to the true and pure Israel represented by the community.[14]

Thus the traditional opposition to the establishment of any other 'house' for God than that which he 'builds' in his people takes a novel form, that of a holy community pointedly describing itself in terms of the symbolic complex associated with the Temple in Jerusalem. 'The transference of this complex of ideas from the temple to the community', Gärtner observes,

may have been facilitated by the fact that even in the Old Testament Israel was sometimes spoken of as 'the house of God,' thus providing a parallel to the ideology of the Qumran community in speaking of itself as 'the house of God,' the true temple. The word 'house' has of course a double meaning: on the one hand 'building,' on the other 'family,' 'dynasty.' In its former meaning it is often used to refer to the temple. This 'house' symbolism seems to have been primary; the symbolism of the 'temple' developed later in response to the demands of a particular situation, in which there was a strong element of temple criticism.[15]

The 'building' of this new house of God is not by natural fertility, as in the days of Rachel and Leah; once again, what had been a literal fact in the tradition becomes a metaphor: 'The eschatological "house of God" is to be built up by a process of exclusiveness, by the avoidance of contact with the unclean and the preservation of ritual purity within the community.'[16] That the idea of natural fertility is present here, if only vestigially, is indicated by the fact that 'an image connected ... in the Qumran texts with those of the house and the temple is that of the "plantation". The

---

[14] 44, 15–16; see also 90, 155 ff.

[15] 44, 21.

[16] 44, 32.

community is called "an eternal plantation, a holy house for Israel."' Gärtner reports that the combination of the idea of a building with that of a planted field 'seems to have come about merely by chance, and appears to lack special motivation', representing only a mechanical recollection of the combined phrase in Jeremiah.[17] Even so, the thought might seem to be there for the finding that the community is a living building, and holiness the life by which it is 'built up' and flourishes.

A more radical estrangement from the Temple, but one similarly rooted in the traditions of Israel, appears among that group of converts to belief in the crucified and risen Christ for whom Stephen speaks.[18] In Stephen's list of the stiff-necked people's historical apostasies the building of the Temple occupies the penultimate place. 'Our fathers had the tabernacle of witness in the wilderness', Stephen says, and brought it with them into the land they conquered from the peoples

> whom God drave out before the face of our fathers, unto the days of David; who found favour before God, and desired to find a tabernacle for the God of Jacob. But Solomon built him an house. Howbeit the most High dwelleth not in temples made with hands: as saith the prophet [Isa. 66:1–2], Heaven is my throne, and earth is my footstool: what house will ye build me? saith the Lord: or what is the place of my rest? Hath not my hand made all these things? (Acts 7:44–50.)

Whatever the attitude of Jesus himself and his first followers, those for whom Stephen speaks are convinced that God despises

---

[17] 44, 27–8. After noting the places in Jeremiah, Gärtner goes on to suggest another origin for this combination of images: 'If we examine later Jewish expositions on the subject of the holy rock of the temple we find a link between this rock and the ideas of Paradise, the water which gives the world life and fertility and the tree of life. We know that there are references in a number of Qumran texts to the garden of Paradise, to the water of life, and to the trees planted by the springs of the water of life, with their roots in the "primeval waters"; and all are connected with the foundation and the eternal future of the community . . . In two of these texts we find related images drawn from the holy building, the house of God (I QH vi and I QS xi). It thus seems likely that the combination of temple and "plantation" in the Qumran texts is to be traced back to Jewish speculations on the subject of the rock of the temple and Paradise.' Perhaps the fact that these speculations involved this particular combination of images may in turn be traced back to the cultural origins suggested here.

[18] Abram Spiro appears to have demonstrated that Stephen speaks for Samaritan converts who find in the Gospel confirmation of their long-standing opposition to the centralization of the cult in Jerusalem. Spiro's argument is summarized in The Anchor Bible Acts of the Apostles (78, 285–300).

the edifice in Jerusalem and dwells among them, his people, as of old. Thus Gärtner is able to assert that

The bond which binds together Qumran and the New Testament is un-doubtedly the intense self-consciousness of the two communities represented; both considered themselves to have been set up in oppo-sition to the temple of the old covenant and its cultus; both believed themselves to have replaced the old temple, for in both the community was the temple.[19]

Similarity on this last specific point, however—the conception of the community itself as temple—, only becomes demonstrable in the New Testament with the work of Paul.[20] Before Paul's con-version all that can be said with certainty is that the traditions which people like Stephen look back to in their rejection of the Temple are like those from which the Essenes derive their con-ception of the community itself as actually replacing the Temple. If the one group found that conception implicit in the traditions of Israel concerning 'houses' and 'building', the other may have found it too; but it is only in the work of Paul, or in places showing his influence, that the symbolism of house and temple is clearly used to describe the Christian community.

In Paul's thought this symbolism is transformed, like every-

[19] 44, 99.

[20] The closest pre-Pauline approach to this conception in the New Testament is in the words of Jesus to Peter in Matthew 16:18: 'And I say also unto thee, That thou art Peter, and upon this rock I will build my church; and the gates of hell shall not prevail against it.' The last part of this saying shows clear affinity with the language of the Dead Sea Scrolls (see Pfammatter (90, 156–7), citing O. Betz, 'Felsenmann und Felsengemeinde. Eine Parallele zu Mt 16. 17–19 in den Qumranpsalmen', *Zeitschrift für die neutestamentliche Wissen-schaft*, 48 (1957), 49–77). Whether the rock is understood to be Peter himself or the belief which he has just confessed, the object of 'I will build' (οἰκοδομήσω) is the people who are to be 'edified' by being taught that belief. Karl Holl observes, 'Daraus ersieht man bereits: die Urgemeinde betrachtet sich selbst als einen gottgegründeten Bau und sieht dies dadurch verbürgt, daß bestimmte, noch lebende Persönlichkeiten von Christus dazu berufen sind, ihren Bestand zu sichern' (56, II, 46). Taken together with the words attributed to Jesus by his accusers, 'I will destroy this temple that is made with hands, and within three days I will build another made without hands' (Mark 14:58), this saying invites interpretation to the effect that the people gathered together by belief in Christ constitute the new Temple. However, this interpretation cannot be established in such a way as to make Matthew 16:18 admissible as historical evidence that the conception of the community as the new Temple was current among the followers of Jesus before Paul. See C. E. B. Cranfield, Commentary (30, 441–2).

thing else, by the mystery of Christ's death and resurrection.[21] The Christian community is not formed simply by the baptismal cleansing of those who join it and their commitment to purity in ritual and life; it is formed by baptism into the death and new life of Christ. The Christian community has its communal identity in Christ. This identification of a collectivity with a single figure recalls the Old Testament manner of recounting the affairs of the tribe as those of an individual, the patriarch; as Gärtner says, 'we have every reason to regard Jesus in the light of the common Jewish principle that the individual can represent the collective, the people'.[22] That principle is decisively modified, however, by being combined with another kind of identification of divers individuals with a single figure. The Apostle to the Gentiles conceives of the people's identity with their Messiah in a manner analogous

[21] 'The thought-world in which the temple symbolism of the New Testament was placed had one unique feature: that Jesus, the founder of the Church, was believed to be the Messiah, and that this Messiah had died and risen again from the dead as the Son of God. And since Jesus was believed to be the Son of God, who now lived with the Father and whose Spirit constituted the Church, all things were centred upon him. True, the Qumran community had its Teacher of Righteousness, the founder of the community and the revealer of the deepest meaning of the Scriptures, but the basis of the community was identical in principle with that of the official Israel—the Law as life and the guarantee of God's blessing in the last days. If it be allowed, then, that Qumran and the New Testament shared the same basic temple symbolism, it must nevertheless be admitted that its "function" and contents differed as between the two groups. Between the temple symbolism of Qumran and that of the New Testament there stands the fact of faith in Jesus as the Messiah and the Son of God. Therefore the distinguishing feature of the temple symbolism of the New Testament is that it depends entirely upon this faith in Jesus. Jewish ideas about the "new" temple were given a new substance in the person of Christ' (Gärtner (44, 101)).

Nevertheless, Johannes Pedersen's description of the manner in which the community was conceptually identified with the ancestor suggests how ready the communal traditions of Israel were to receive this 'new substance': 'The relation to the fathers becomes common life. . . . What the fathers have handed down is inherited by the generations, and the experiences of the latter act in the fathers; therefore the responsibility is a common one. It is a thought with which we are constantly confronted in the prophets: the people bear the blessing of the fathers, but also their guilt. All events are connected, because they contribute towards forming a psychic whole, into which they are merged. Thus there rises out of the history of the people an invisible figure of grand proportions, bearing the impress of definite features, the features left by experiences. And this figure is identical with the ancestor' (85, 475–6). With this observation cf. that of H. H. Rowley (Introduction, p. xiv, n. 14 above); both may be said to describe the emergence in the Bible of an 'idiographic' order in the sense defined in Chapter I, pp. 16–17 above.

[22] 44, 122.

to that in which the celebrants of a pagan mystery are identified with their dying and reborn deity. Thus the Christian community is never called the 'house of Christ', as the Old Testament alone might have suggested; it is Christ's body, formed by the new life of its members in Christ.

Paul thus introduces into the complex of Jewish traditional motifs concerning collective identity a conception suggested by the Hellenic mystery cults, thereby bringing out an implication in Old Testament patterns of thought which the Essene community comes short of realizing. The traditional manner of contrasting the house built of wood and stone with the house 'built' by the genera-tion of life in the people now comes to suggest the idea of a com-munity constituted, not by its visible institutions or its locality, or even by blood relationship or common traditions, but by a mysterious life permeating it. When Paul tells the Church in Corinth, 'ye are God's husbandry, ye are God's building' (1 Cor. 3:9), the association of building with planting is no longer an otiose formula, as it appears to be in the Essene texts; it has the full significance which, in retrospect, can be seen to have been adumbrated by Jeremiah when he set off the building and planting of the people against the destruction of the city and the Temple.

The new significance of the combined metaphor is beautifully expressed in the Epistle to the Ephesians, where it is used to describe the incorporation of Gentiles into the 'household of God':

Now therefore ye are no more strangers and foreigners (πάροικοι), but fellow citizens with the saints, and of the household (οἰκεῖοι) of God: and are built (ἐποικοδομηθέντες) upon the foundation of the apostles and prophets, Jesus Christ himself being the chief corner stone; in whom all the building (οἰκοδομή) fitly framed together groweth into a holy temple in the Lord: in whom ye also are builded together (συνοικο-δομεῖσθε) for an habitation (κατοικτήριον) of God through the Spirit.[23]

The root-idea of 'house', οἶκος, runs through this passage and in the course of it undergoes a change. The word πάροικοι, 'foreign-ers', would seem to have been used solely for the purpose of intro-ducing it, since the word adds little otherwise to the sense of ξένοι,

---

[23] Eph. 2:19–22. The question whether Paul wrote this epistle is not relevant to the present purpose, except as a way of asking what the connection is between the ideas and metaphorical usages here and those of indisputably Pauline pas-sages like 1 Corinthians 12.

'strangers'. The idea of the Church as the house of God is contained in οἰκεῖοι, and such is the forward pressure of thought in the passage that, when in the next instant the human members of the household become the materials of which the house itself is built, the change seems less a mixed metaphor than a metamorphosis. Although at first it might seem that living people had become frozen, like Niobe, into stone, it soon appears that, on the contrary, the building has become a living, growing thing. Its human materials participate in a living unity: συνοικοδομεῖσθε should probably read as a middle rather than a passive, for this building is not so much something that is done to or with the materials as it is something that happens spontaneously within them and among them. Precious as this living unity is to those who participate in it, however, it does not exist for its own sake but for God, and the passage ends as it began, with the thought of the Church as God's dwelling.

To describe the social order of the Christian community further, these two metaphors—'building' and 'planting'—are combined with a third, the most important of all. As the living temple of God comes into being by its members' participation in the life of the risen Christ, so the idea that Christians are 'one body in Christ' (Rom. 12:5) supplies the basic metaphor describing its social form.[24] To describe—and justify—the social order by comparing the various classes to the members of a human body is a Greco-Roman commonplace, best known from the fable of Menenius Agrippa.[25] Thus, while Paul owes to the Old Testament his sense of the opposition between the living temple and all such structures as men can build by their own devices, it is the Hellenic side of his world that supplies him with a *topos* for describing the actual shape of the building, the harmony of its form:

For the body is not one member, but many. If the foot shall say, Because I am not the hand, I am not of the body; is it therefore not of the

---

[24] The word σῶμα does not appear in pre-Christian usage with the meaning of 'society' or 'collectivity'. Cerfaux, *The Church* (18, 272–3), reviews a scholarly controversy on this point leading to the conclusion stated by F. De Visscher (*Les Édits d'Auguste*, p. 91): 'In spite of all our research it has proved impossible to discover a single example in which this word designates a collectivity. Σῶμα means a unity, a whole, but never a collectivity. And I think that I can assert that this meaning is not a Greek one.'

[25] Ernest Best provides a concise account of the history of the metaphor before Paul in *One Body in Christ* (7, 221–5).

body? And if the ear shall say, Because I am not the eye, I am not of the body; is it therefore not of the body? If the whole body were an eye, where were the hearing? If the whole were hearing, where were the smelling? But now hath God set the members every one of them in the body, as it hath pleased him. And if they were all one member, where were the body? But now are they many members, yet but one body. And the eye cannot say unto the hand, I have no need of thee: nor again the head to the feet, I have no need of you. Nay, much more those members of the body, which seem to be more feeble, are necessary: And those members of the body, which we think to be less honourable, upon these we bestow more abundant honour; and our uncomely parts have more abundant comeliness. For our comely parts have no need: but God hath tempered the body together, having given more abundant honour to that part which lacked: that there should be no schism in the body; but that the members should have the same care one for another. And whether one member suffer, all the members suffer with it; or one member be honoured, all the members rejoice with it. Now ye are the body of Christ and members in particular (1 Cor. 12:14–27).

Paul uses the *topos* to 'bestow more abundant honour' on the humble members of the Christian community; in the fable of Menenius it is used to keep them in their place—La Fontaine succinctly points the moral:

> ... Ménénius leur fit voir
> Qu'ils étaient aux membres semblables,
> Et par cet apologue, insigne entre les fables,
> Les ramena dans leur devoir.

This difference in the use made of the comparison arises from an even more basic difference between the conception of society which Paul takes the *topos* to express and that which it has always expressed before this time. The primary thing for Paul is not the social order itself which the comparison with a human body describes, but the life manifested by that order:

Now there are diversities of gifts, but the same Spirit.... And there are diversities of operations, but it is the same God which worketh all in all. But the manifestation of the Spirit is given to every man to profit withal (1 Cor. 12:4, 6–7).

Because it is the same Spirit that animates the whole body, those members with humbler gifts possess the essential thing that makes gifts valuable, and those with higher gifts cannot glory in their superiority.

This use of the *topos* to put order itself in its place, so to speak, is new. Before Paul the comparison of society to a human body had been used to assert the need for social order, but what might seem its most obvious point had never been drawn: that order in society must result from something analogous to the power of life which produces the structure of a living body.[26] This is precisely what is conveyed in the Old Testament pattern of thought centring on the motif of 'building and planting'. The contrast between the two kinds of 'building' begins in simple nomadic distrust of the structures of settled civilization, and issues in the thought that the temples men construct only figure forth the true temple which God builds for himself by the Spirit of life in his people. In the synthesis of Paul's thought this conception combines with a Greek *topos* for order which, before this interaction between Jewish and Greek thought, appears strangely lifeless.

As the fact of Christ's death and resurrection is at the centre of Paul's belief, so this complex of metaphors centres on the ideas of death and of life and of the relation between dead or non-living things and living ones. That edification follows as growth from a planting cannot be fully understood without recalling Paul's description of the believers' participation in Christ's death as a planting:

For if we have been planted together in the likeness of his death, we shall be also in the likeness of his resurrection . . . (Rom. 6:5).

The death into 'newness of life' in Christ is a new kind of birth, and the Church's edification is a new kind of coming of age. It will go on

Till we all come in the unity of the faith, and of the knowledge of the Son of God, unto a perfect man, unto the measure of the stature of the fulness of Christ: That we henceforth be no more children, tossed to and fro, and carried about with every wind of doctrine, by the sleight of men, and cunning craftiness, whereby they lie in wait to deceive; But speaking the truth in love, may grow up into him in all things, which is the head, even Christ: From whom the whole body fitly joined together and compacted by that which every joint supplieth, according to the

[26] 'In Paul's writings there is a mystical theory of life in Christ which transformed the Hellenistic simile of the body and its members. From now on this simile signifies more than just unity: it tells us that unity is brought about by the one life of Christ which animates all Christians as if they were—or rather, who are—all members of the body of Christ' (Cerfaux, 18, 267).

effectual working in the measure of every part, maketh increase of the body unto the edifying (οἰκοδομὴν) of itself in love (Eph. 4:13–16).

That body, whose inner life is evoked more effectively here than in any other single passage, is the ultimate form of humanity. The edification of the individual and that of the collectivity are one and the same process, which comes about by virtue of the death and resurrection of Christ. In both it is identification with Christ that changes dead and disordered materials into something that lives and grows towards its perfect form.

The change is both more mysterious and more distinctly conceived than any simple influx of something non-physical into the physical. The very fact that this is so means that the relation between the changed materials and their material environment is complicated. The nature of this complication is most clearly expressed in terms of its effect on the principle of Christian liberty in the use of such things as had formerly seemed to possess some benign or malignant virtue in themselves but are now seen to be 'weak and beggarly elements' (τὰ ἀσθενῆ καὶ πτωχὰ στοιχεῖα— Gal. 4:9), so that it makes no difference whether they are used or not. A person living in faith may move about confidently in the world of such things, using them for the various purposes of life, or leaving them alone if they serve no purpose. He need not fear them. Indeed, he must not fear them, for that would mean that he was falling back into bondage to them; but to notice that danger is to realize that these things, having lost their former powers, have taken on a new kind of power, or one newly understood. It may be described as the power of reassimilating the living creature into the dead world where dead things have a kind of life, or a kind of power against life.[27] Thus Christian liberty is not simply a release;

---

[27] This meaning need not be affected by the possibility that the στοιχεῖα may be specifically associated, by way of demonology, with the angels who delivered the law to Moses, according to a Rabbinic tradition referred to by Paul in Galatians 3:19. Albert Schweitzer interprets Paul's idea of freedom from the law in these terms: 'By means of the Law men were placed in pupilage to the World-Elements (τὰ στοιχεῖα τοῦ κόσμου, Gal. iv.3,9), who kept them in dependence upon themselves, until God, through Christ, set them free from the curse of the Law (Gal. iv.1–5). Accordingly when those who had been heathens submitted themselves as Christians to the Law this means, according to Paul, nothing else than that, instead of serving solely the one God, they once more (though in another form) submit themselves to the World-Elements, now rendered powerless by Christ, observing the "days, months, seasons, and years" which belong to their service (Gal. iv.8–11)' (105, 70). Sixteenth-century

rather, it is an active engagement in a struggle like that of organic life to resist dissolution. The exercise of Christian liberty is subject to constraints analogous to those by which life is conditioned on pain of ceasing to be.

In 1 Corinthians the connection between this dynamic of liberty and Paul's distinctive idea of communal order is established by a single verbal clue. The description of the harmonious co-operation of the members of the body concludes with the famous words:

> But covet earnestly the best gifts: and yet shew I unto you a more excellent way. Though I speak with the tongues of men and of angels, and have not charity, I am become as sounding brass or a tinkling cymbal. And though I have the gift of prophecy, and understand all mysteries, and have all knowledge; and though I have all faith, so that I could remove mountains, and not have charity, I am nothing. And though I bestow all my goods to feed the poor, and though I give my body to be burned, and have not charity, it profiteth me nothing. Charity suffereth long, and is kind; charity envieth not; charity vaunteth not itself, is not puffed up ...

Charity has been spoken of once before in this Epistle; then, as here, it is described by contrast with a gift which 'puffeth up': 'Now as touching things offered unto idols, we know that we all have knowledge. Knowledge puffeth up, but charity edifieth' (8:1). This concise formula summarizes the argument which follows, in which Paul subjects the freedom that he has vindicated for Christians to a communal imperative:

> As concerning therefore the eating of those things that are offered in sacrifice unto idols, we know that an idol is nothing in the world, and that there is none other God but one. . . . Howbeit there is not in every man that knowledge: for some with conscience of the idol unto this hour eat it as a thing offered unto an idol; and their conscience being weak is defiled. But meat commendeth us not to God: for neither, if we eat, are we the better; neither, if we eat not, are we the worse. But take heed lest by any means this liberty of yours become a stumblingblock to them that are weak. For if any man see thee which hast knowledge sit at meat in the idol's temple, shall not the conscience of him which is weak be emboldened (οἰκοδομηθήσεται) to eat those things which are offered to idols; and through thy knowledge shall the weak brother perish, for whom Christ died? But when ye sin so against the brethren,

---

Puritans, taking the στοιχεῖα to be whatever shows the strange power of non-life against spiritual life, may be said to arrive at a 'demythologized' understanding of Paul's meaning.

and wound their weak conscience, ye sin against Christ. Wherefore, if meat make my brother to offend, I will eat no flesh while the world standeth, lest I make my brother to offend.

The disregard of conscience to which the weak brother will be emboldened, or literally 'edified', by the example of the strong is a silly travesty of true Christian liberty, and the 'edification' thus accomplished is a caricature of the real communication of that knowledge which makes Christians free. Exercised in scorn of those who do not possess it, the gift of knowledge does not 'build' but 'puffeth up', like the frog in Aesop who tried to swell to the size of the ox. Similarly, all the other gifts whose operation is described by the comparison of the community to a human body have their true value only as communal functions, only as they serve to 'edify' the Christian community:

How is it then, brethren? when ye come together, every one of you hath a psalm, hath a doctrine, hath a tongue, hath a revelation, hath an interpretation. Let all things be done unto edifying (1 Cor. 14:26).

Thus the verb 'to edify' connects the idea of the Christian community as formed by the harmonious use of spiritual gifts with the topic of Christian liberty in the use of meat from animals sacrificed to pagan idols.

Elizabethan Puritans and Conformists alike see in this question of the use of 'idolothytes' the biblical analogue to the question of sacerdotal vestments. The rival analogy which might seem to offer itself between the popish vestments and the priestly trappings described in the Old Testament is rejected by both sides: by Conformists in order to forestall the charge, which Milton brings against them in *The Reason of Church Government*, of retreating from Christ to a literal reinstatement of the 'shadowy types' of Christ in the Aaronic priesthood;[28] by Puritans because they refuse to grant the same honour to the inventions of the Roman Antichrist as to the institutions of God in the Old Testament.[29] Thus both

---

[28] 'Last of all, who seeth not that these few orders, now to be observed, are not enjoined as figures or shadows of anything to come: but as some means (if it might be for a time) to set forward the building of God' (83, Sig. 4* 4).

[29] 'It is a good saying, to this purpose, that the old mother Synagogue was to be buried with honour. But we owe no such honour to the *Roman* Antichrist. God did appoint Circumcision and other Ceremonies to the Jewish church: but that whore of *Babylon*, that made all the Kings of the earth drunken with her golden cup and painted colours, appointed these trifles to her bastardly brood' (48, Sig. G7ᵛ).

sides decline what might seem to be the most obvious biblical analogy, and instead take the wearing of the surplice and square cap to be the equivalent of eating meats known to have been consecrated to idols before being sold in the market. 'Now mark this matter that we have in hand' says Anthony Gilby's 'Soldier of Barwick' to an old companion-in-arms turned 'English Chaplain':

These popish gear were Idolothytes, things belonging to Idols, in the wearing whereof, many good men's consciences are offended, and they openly tell you, that they were things wherein the Idols were served, and that they are grieved to see you wear such liveries of Antichrist, & so they are offended in Charity, and cannot use you as Brethren as they were wont to do. Again, the papists, and the weaker sort, that have not been fully taught, do still think and say, and teach others, that these are the things that belonged to their Mass, and to other popish idolatry, and therefore all the popery was not evil, seeing Christ's Ministers and Sacraments cannot be without them. Thus their weak consciences are offended in faith, and think their old idolatry good, and therefore cannot repent of it. Wherefore for the consciences of others (if there were no cause else) you should abstain from this liberty, that you challenge to yourselves, in these idolatrous garments, like as Paul affirmeth, that he would never eat flesh, rather than he should be thought, willingly and wittingly being once warned, to eat any meat dedicated to Idols.[30]

Conformists reply to all this by pointing out that offence is sometimes taken where none has really been given. This distinction, already a commonplace in Continental reformers' treatment of such questions as whether to eat meat on Friday, takes on a novel twist in England. With respect to eating meat on Friday, for example, the distinction between an offence given and one merely taken comes down to a question of the motives and underlying spiritual condition of the parties, which may not always be easy to determine. 'If you do anything with unseemly levity, or wantonness, or rashness, out of its proper order or place,' Calvin says, 'so as to cause the ignorant and the simple to stumble, such will be called an offense given by you. . . .' On the other hand,

An offense is spoken of as received when something, otherwise not wickedly or unseasonably committed, is by ill will or malicious intent of mind wrenched into occasion for offense. . . . Accordingly, we shall call the one the offense of the weak, the other that of the Pharisees. Thus we

[30] 48, Sig. E7 and verso.

shall so temper the use of our freedom as to allow for the ignorance of our weak brothers, but for the rigor of the Pharisees, not at all![31]

In England, with respect to 'idolatrous garments', the question becomes much simpler. Psychological complexities cease where law 'takes order': 'But concerning the offending of the weak,' says Matthew Parker, 'briefly':

> In indifferent things, if law for common tranquility have prescribed no order what ought to be done, a Christian man ought to have a great regard of his neighbor's conscience, according to St. Paul's doctrine. But if law foreseeing harms and providing quietness, have taken lawful order therein, offence is taken, and not given, when the subject doth his duty in obedience, so severely enjoined him by God's word.[32]

The good Pauline text, 'Let every soul be subject unto the higher powers' (Rom. 13:1), cuts this Gordian knot in Tudor England. The English situation is like what Paul's would have been if an edict had gone out from a benevolent emperor requiring, for the sake of good order, that Christians should always eat meats offered to idols.

Elizabeth's policy with respect to Church vestments was in effect an ingenious use of the principle of Christian liberty to tame the English Reformation. She allowed her Church to preach as purely reformed doctrine as it pleased, on condition that it should act in a manner admittedly reminiscent of the Roman cult with respect to certain indifferent things like surplices, tippets, and square caps. For a time the Reformers could bemuse themselves with the thought that the inscrutable young woman on the throne was leading the country into the light gently. 'I know that all changes of importance in the state are offensive and disagreeable,' John Jewel explained to Peter Martyr, 'and that many things are often tolerated by sovereigns by reason of the times. And this at first, probably, was not attended with inconvenience; but now that the full light of the gospel has shone forth, the very vestiges of error must, as far as possible, be removed together with the rubbish, and, as the saying is, with the very dust.'[33] But, to alter the saying, Elizabeth continued to insist that the bath be kept with the baby, and the Reformers made the choice that seemed to them

[31] 15, 843: III, xix, 11.
[32] 83, Sig. 3* 3ᵛ.
[33] 93, 100.

indicated by the principles of Christian liberty and edification. As Edmund Grindal later explained,

We, who are now bishops, on our first return, and before we entered on our ministry, contended long and earnestly for the removal of those things that have occasioned the present dispute; but as we were unable to prevail, either with the queen or the parliament, we judged it best, after a consultation on the subject, not to desert our churches for the sake of a few ceremonies, and those not unlawful in themselves, especially since the pure doctrine of the gospel remained in all its integrity and freedom. . . .[34]

Or, as Parker tells the anti-vestiarian ministers with somewhat more asperity, 'you require *freedom to teach your flocks by doctrine.* This thing your bonded obedience may easily obtain: whereas by your own willfulness, you deprive yourselves thereof.'[35] Once civil power has commanded the wearing of certain vestments, Whitgift explains, they become by that very fact necessary to edification:

For you know that it is an order and law in the church of England, that none should either administer the sacraments or preach, except he receive the apparel appointed: forasmuch therefore as he that refuseth to wear the apparel, by order of this church, may not preach, and therefore cannot that way 'edify;' and he that weareth that apparel may preach, and so 'edify,' therefore the apparel, *per accidens*, doth 'edify;' even as the church, the pulpit, and other such things do. . . .[36]

The situation in which Elizabeth placed her churchmen required them to limit the meaning of edification to the imparting of doctrine.

Thus Conformist usage of the word 'to edify' tends to approximate to the simple sense which the word has today of imparting a message calculated to improve the hearer. There appears in the Conformists' replies to their opponents a certain impatience with the trouble that is being stirred up over such an elementary idea. Thus Parker writes:

The first discourse here is of edifying or building the Church of Christ, which all faithful Ministers do acknowledge to be their bounden duty and service, according to the graces of God bestowed upon them,

[34] 93, 169.
[35] 83, Sig. 7* 1ᵛ–7* 2.
[36] 120, I, 71.

and never to hinder and pluck down a whit: whereof much more might be said than is here rehearsed, if it were needful to wade further in so worthy a matter.

The word 'worthy' seems awkward; the context calls for a word to explain why it is not needful to wade further in the matter, and perhaps something like 'obvious' was what Parker was on the point of saying. Edification seems to the Conformist a fairly commonplace notion, and he would be puzzled by the way his opponents carry on about it if he did not have a partisan explanation ready to hand:

Wherewithal in texts and expositions, you would not greatly have enlarged your books, if it had not been to make all God's workmen saving yourselves suspected to the world, as pluckers down and destroyers of God's most holy Temple, builded upon the foundation of the Apostles and Prophets: when as through the grace of God working in them by true and sound doctrine in this apparel and orders, many earnest labourers of the Lord's do travail to bring his people to the full knowledge of Christ, howsoever you have entangled and encumbered the consciences of your hearers.[37]

Why the Puritans should choose the theme of edification particularly as the vehicle for this self-interested attack on the Establishment Parker does not try to guess. Dean John Bridges, however, evidently sees all this Puritan talk about 'building' as an instance of his opponents' rather naive manner of dwelling upon scriptural metaphor. The passage of arch reiteration in which he conveys his amusement represents the sort of thing that prompted Martin Marprelate to answer Bridges in kind as a fellow clown:

... indeed we tell them plainly that they *build* not well: but both hinder and overthrow their *brethren's building*: yea, they contrary and hinder their own *building*. And most fain would we have them leave this strange manner of *building*: but not utterly to leave all manner of *building*: but to join with us whom they confess to be their *brethren*, that we *build* on rock also, and for all material parts and substance of the *building*, they say, they agree with us. And we *builded*, and *builded well*, before they began, or were able to lay a stone or temper mortar to this *building*.[38]

Bridges' serious point is that 'building' is, after all, only a figurative expression. Since the Puritans say they agree with their conforming brethren in 'all material parts and substance' of edification,

[37] 83, Sig. 2* 3^v–2* 4.   [38] 10, 10.

which is to say in doctrine, they should moderate their raptures about 'building' and concentrate on the work of edification in the straightforward, literal sense of the word: to impart doctrine.

For the Conformist, then, both Christian liberty and edification are matters of inward understanding. Together they describe an integrity of conscience maintained by a conscious disjunction between social gesture and inner meaning, between metaphor and sober sense:

As touching Christian liberty, the faithful man must know, that it is altogether spiritual, and pertaineth only to the conscience, which must be pacified concerning the law of God, and next well stayed in things indifferent. This liberty consisteth herein, not to be holden & tied with any religion in external things; but that it may be lawful before God to use them or omit them, as occasion shall serve. This persuasion a godly man must always retain & keep safe in his mind: but when he cometh to the use & action of them, then must he moderate and qualify his liberty, according to charity toward his neighbour, and obedience to his Prince. So though by this knowledge his mind and conscience is always free: yet his doing is as it were tied or limited by law or love. Whereupon a well learned man [Calvin] saith: it is sufficient in Christian liberty to understand, that before God it is no matter, what meats or what clothes thou use, though in thy whole life thou never eat flesh, and though always after thou use in apparel one colour, and fashion. . . . Now then forasmuch as these garments are among things indifferent, we may easily know how they are free as pertaining to our conscience, and yet notwithstanding we may be obedient to laws without impairing of Christian liberty.[39]

Following the unexceptionable exegetic principle of bringing one place in scripture to bear on another, the Conformist inserts Paul's precept about obedience to the higher powers into the complex of liberty, charity, and edification; and at a stroke the whole complex becomes clear. It is seen to describe an admirable combination of inner integrity, civil obedience, and mutual forbearance, applicable not only to conduct in church, after all, but to any Christian, or indeed any civilized, social intercourse.

In contrast, the tract which Parker is answering, Robert Crowley's *Briefe discourse against the outwarde apparrell . . .*, defies paraphrase:

First, we consider that the power that God hath given to his Ministers is given them that they should thereby edify or build up the Church of

Christ, & not destroy it, or pull it down: according as S. Paul writeth to the Corinths. Of which edifying or building of the church of Christ, the same S. Paul speaketh in that Epistle that he wrote to the Ephesians. . . .

First he saith thus, *Iam non estis hospites, &c.* Ye are not now strangers and foreigners, but ye are Citizens together with the saints, and of the household of God being builded upon the foundation of the Apostles & Prophets, Jesus Christ being the Head stone in the corner. In whom whatsoever building is increased it groweth into an holy temple in the Lord. These words doth S. Paul write to signify that the church of Christ, which is builded of living stones & timber taken out both from among the Jews and the gentiles, must be builded upon the firm & sure foundation Jesus Christ, & not upon any other (for he was that foundation that the Apostles & Prophets builded upon) and that the building which is set upon the foundation doth grow into an holy Temple in the Lord. The builders must not suffer it to decay, but they must still labour diligently, that it may grow into an holy temple, and that till it be as large & as beautiful as it is possible for it to be in this vale of misery. So far off would S. Paul have all the builders of God's temple to be from the pulling down or defacing any part thereof.[40]

Crowley's vision centres on the unique idea of the living temple. His argument against the required 'outward apparel' of the clergy derives its imperative force from the biblical antithesis between 'building' and 'destruction', growth and dissolution. No third possibility appears for him between these two processes: whatever does not build destroys; the temple either grows or dies. When Christian liberty is conceived of within this metaphorical context, it means the ascendency of life in the building; its converse is a sinking back of the communal body toward subjection to things without life, to idols. This distinctive communal concept is the starting point of Puritanism as it defines itself in the vestiarian controversy.

Thus the fact that Elizabethan Puritanism developed its programme concerning fundamental Church polity out of an initial preoccupation with Christian liberty in the use of indifferent things gives a special character to the Puritan discussion of the Church. The question of the nature of Church offices is closely associated in Puritan thought with the Pauline imperative of edification. The passages in the Epistles from which the Puritans, like Bucer and Calvin before them, claim to deduce scriptural prescriptions for

---

[40] 31, Sig. Aii^v–Aiii.

Church offices are those in which Paul is urging the need for co-operation among people possessing different spiritual gifts:

And he gave some, apostles; and some, prophets; and some evangelists; and some, pastors and teachers; For the perfecting of the saints, for the work of the ministry, for the edifying of the body of Christ . . . (Eph. 4:11–12).

Such passages supply Bucer and Calvin and the English Puritans with the point of departure for a process of logical deduction, perhaps plausible but certainly uninspiring, out of which emerge certain eternally prescribed Church offices; however, these are also the passages which convey the Pauline vision of the Church as a '. . . whole body fitly joined together and compacted by that which every joint supplieth, according to the effectual working in the measure of every part . . . unto the edifying of itself in love' (4:16). While Calvin appreciates the figurative force of such a passage, it appeals to him principally as showing that the 'human ministry which God uses to govern the church is the chief sinew by which believers are held together in one body'.[41] In contrast to this stress on the need of ministerial sinew to hold the members of the body together, English Puritanism begins with the 'effectual working' of the process of edification itself. The English readily adopt their Continental mentors' arguments from scripture concerning Church offices, but they bring to them a conviction which derives its force in a special manner from Paul's vision of a living Church.

The special force of this Pauline idea for Puritans results from the fact that the English situation serves to focus attention on the relationship between two distinct topics in Paul's Epistles: the meaning of Christian liberty and the need for co-operation among people possessing different gifts.[42] These two topics are obviously related in the general sense that both concern the communal life of the Church, but the only indication that Paul gives of a closer connection between them is, as has been seen, that the verb 'to edify' and its derivatives appear in his discussions of both these topics and, it may be added, of no others. When he is urging the need for

[41] 15, 1055: IV, iii, 2.
[42] To have seen this connection and worked out its implications may be called the distinctive contribution of Puritanism to the interpretation of Paul. Even those modern studies which correspond most closely to the Puritan understanding of Paul's theology of the Church in other respects (e.g., Cerfaux (18), Best (7), and Pfammater (90)) do not observe this connection or the contrast which follows from it between the communal order of the Church and any other social order.

co-operation, Paul uses the classical metaphor comparing the social classes to the members of a body; when he is explaining to his converts how they should use their Christian liberty with respect to 'idolothytes', he evokes the thought of the constant struggle of the 'new creature' to assert and sustain its new life amid the old, non-living things. By drawing these two topics together, Elizabethan Puritans discover that the social order which results from the operation of the Spirit of life is opposed not merely to disorder but, more significantly, to a non-living kind of order.

Elizabeth committed her Church to the principle that order is to be established by the regulation of indifferent things. The very fact that such things as vestments and ceremonies possess no spiritual value in themselves is precisely what makes them available for use in establishing order. Once established, that order can become a vehicle of the Spirit. Bishop Bancroft expands Whitgift's formula of edification '*per accidens*' into a basic Conformist theory of the relationship between material order and spiritual life:

For in proper speech the holy ghost doth only edify by the ministry of his word: and yet edification which is ascribed to ceremonies, is but *per accidens*: as when men being brought through order and decency in the Church to a more reverent behaviour and opinion of divine Service, they are by God's spirit the sooner edified. For ceremonies therefore to be orderly and decent, is their tending to edification: and none other edifying can proceed from them, but as they be both decent and orderly.[43]

The Conformist thinks of edification as subsequent to order. When the vessel has been shaped, the Spirit, he trusts, will come to fill it. If the Puritan objects, in Pauline phrase, that 'to know what can edify & build anything, it is necessary to bring things of like substance. For chaff, straw, and stubble cannot build nor edify with any precious metal: carnal things cannot make the perfect building of things spiritual',[44] the Conformist replies, in effect, that 'chaff, straw, and stubble' (1 Cor. 3:12) can be considered to edify '*per accidens*', God willing.

In contrast, the Puritan thinks of order in the Church as coming into being by the process of edification. As the individual member of the body grows in the strength of his new life in Christ, he communicates that strength to others, while always taking care lest in

[43] 5, 39.
[44] 48, Sig. H7.

his own assurance he frighten weaker consciences back toward the old state of comfortable bondage to the 'dead and beggarly elements'. By this interaction of consciences the Church emerges in the midst of civil society, just as a living organism grows in an environment which both threatens and nourishes it. Its form springs from this intercommunication of the Spirit among the members; its offices are functions of this process. Since these functions are mentioned by Paul in his descriptions of harmony among the members of Christ's body, the offices which they define can confidently be taken for the natural features of the living Church. To say that this Church order is established by the Word can thus amount to much the same thing as saying that it is created by the Spirit. This living order struggles to disengage itself from structures contrived by human wit and imposed by civil policy just as the individual conscience struggles to free itself from the support offered by prescribed observances.

Dismemberment will cause the destruction of this living body, however, and Puritans are sensitive to the charge that by taking offence at the idolothytic garments they are moving toward Separatism. Their only reply is to say that the living temple can also be destroyed by being held together in the wrong way. These two kinds of destruction correspond to the two kinds of 'offence' described by Anthony Gilby's Soldier of Barwick, and the Puritan is quick to point out that the argument that 'offence' can be taken as well as given pertains to only one of the two. It concerns only those who are actually complaining about the idolothytes; it disregards 'the papists, and the weaker sort', whose consciences are 'offended' by being pleased. The Conformist's way of dealing with this matter, Cartwright complains,

procedeth of too foul an oversight and want of understanding of the word *offence*, for Saint Paul by offence doth not mean displeasure or discontentment: but that whereby occasion is given to any of sin and transgression of the law of God, which may as well be with allowance as disallowance, when all are pleased with that which is done as when they are displeased.[45]

A conscience is 'offended' by being encouraged either in superstitious dependence on 'indifferent things' or in the kind of in-

souciant travesty of Christian liberty that Paul's ironic usage in
1 Corinthians 8:10 refers to:

Again, although I have knowledge, and know that the wearing of a surplice is lawful for me, yet another which hath not knowledge is by my
example edified or strengthened to wear a surplice, whereof he can tell
no ground why he should wear it, and so sinneth against his conscience:
and for this cause St Paul concludeth, that that which a man may do in
respect of himself may not be done, and is not lawful to be done, in
respect of other.[46]

To be sure, the simple soul who 'can tell no ground' why he
should wear the surplice can be told he should wear it as commanded by the civil authority for the sake of order. The Puritan's
dissatisfaction with that solution really arises from dissatisfaction
with the kind of order it implies for the Church. It implies order
imposed from without, an order constructed by means of 'dead and
beggarly elements', for those are precisely the 'things indifferent'
which Christian liberty makes available for the magistrate to use in
the interest of order, according to the Conformist. The quiet State
which this policy has in view is the antithesis of Church order as
the Puritan conceives it. The kind of harmony that is assured 'when
all are pleased' may signify as surely as any chaos the destruction
of the living temple. It may represent the exact opposite of that
intercommunication of the Spirit of life by which the members of
the body are edified. Thus the vestiarian controversy impels Puritanism toward a conception of the Church as a special kind of social
order, defined by contradistinction from the order established by
civil policy. Cartwright declares:

As for the . . . error or flattery *that in things indifferent commanded by the
Magistrate, we ought not to have such regard to the offence of the weak, but
that if all should be offended,* that is to say perish and make shipwreck of
conscience (for that is the offence which S. Paul and we after him speak
of) *yet we ought to do that which is commanded*: the Magistrate being
thereby lifted above the Lord, we utterly condemn [it]. Considering it
being a flat commandment of the holy ghost that we abstain from things
in their own nature indifferent if the weak brother should be offended,
no authority either of church or commonwealth can make it void.

This prohibition against 'offending' the weak is simply the obverse
of the Puritans' positive insistence on edification. The 'flat com-

[46] 120, II, 4.

mandment' of the Holy Ghost, as Puritans understand it, refers to a principle of harmony among the members of the communal body whereby the strong communicate life to the weak, all growing in that freedom which is the ascendency of life over the 'dead and beggarly elements' of the world. Nothing could be better calculated to throw that principle into clear relief than a 'flat commandment' of the civil magistrate prescribing the use of certain indifferent things for the sake of harmony. Cartwright continues:

And where the magistrate's commanding and our obedience unto him ought to be squared out first by the love of God, then of men, our brethren especially, this new carpenter, as one that frameth his squire according to his timber and not his timber according to the squire, will make our obedience to the civil Magistrate the rule of the love of God and our brethren. So that instead that he should teach that we may obey no further unto the magistrate than the same will agree with the glory of God and salvation of our brethren, he teacheth that in things of their own nature indifferent we must have no further regard neither to salvation of our brethren nor to the glory of God (which in neglect of their salvation is trodden under foot) than will agree with doing that [which] the magistrate commandeth.[47]

The process of edification, the Puritan insists, is by scriptural definition autonomous. The autonomy of the Church is understood as a consequence of this principle. Church and State represent two kinds of order, two kinds of 'building'. To square the edification of the living temple to the order of civil policy is to deny its very nature.

The 'rules' which the Puritans insist that they find in Paul governing 'such cases as are not particularly mentioned of in scripture' refer to this autonomous process of communal life. For the Puritan the meaning of 'edification' and of 'offence', and consequently the meaning of 'order and seemliness' in the Church and of behaviour directed to the glory of God, involves a unique complex of ideas and metaphors. The Conformist is led by the very nature of the Elizabethan settlement to a manner of reading which destroys this vital complex, acknowledging in its operative terms only such meanings as they can retain in general parlance apart from it. Thus Hooker asserts that the four general rules of Church polity which Cartwright cites from Paul are really only

'edicts of nature' which would have been evident to all men everywhere, whether Paul had ever mentioned them or not:

The rules are these, 'Nothing scandalous or offensive unto any, especially unto the Church of God;' 'All things in order and with seemliness;'
'All unto edification;' finally, 'All to the glory of God.' Of which kind
how many might be gathered out of the Scripture, if it were necessary
to take so much pains? Which rules they that urge, minding thereby to
prove that nothing may be done in the Church but what Scripture commandeth, must needs hold that they tie the Church of Christ no otherwise than only because we find them there set down by the finger of the
Holy Ghost. . . .
   The truth is, they are rules and canons of that law which is written in
all men's hearts; the Church had for ever no less than now stood bound
to observe them, whether the Apostle had mentioned them or no.[48]

Hooker's assertion depends entirely on simplifying and general-
izing the meanings of the terms as the Conformist does. In effect,
his argument is circular: if the terms in which these rules are
couched are deprived of their uniquely Pauline functions, then the
rules can be grasped without any necessary reference to Paul. But
when these rules are understood as the Puritan understands them,
it becomes quite meaningless to ask whether they would be binding
if Paul had not mentioned them; without Paul they would not
exist. To say that these Pauline conceptions are simply 'rules and
canons of that law which is written in all men's hearts' is like saying
that the meaning of the *Oresteia* or the *Aeneid*—or of *Don Quixote*
or *Hamlet*—could be gathered simply out of the nature of things
without taking pains to consult those particular works. Such powerfully formative works are undoubtedly 'agreeable to' right reason,
but the general canons of reason do not suffice to comprehend their
meaning. They draw to themselves and transform various and
sometimes disparate commonplaces of their civilization, but their
meaning cannot be resolved into commonplaces. The ideas of
Christian 'liberty', 'edification', and 'offence' interact in the work
of Paul to produce a total conception which the Conformist resolves into the discrete principles that 'thought is free', that pure
doctrine must be taught, and that Christians should bear with each
other's religious susceptibilities wherever possible. He regards
these as reasonable rules, such as 'might be gathered out of

[48] 57, I, 361–2: *Laws*, III, vii, 1–2.

Scripture' in any number 'if it were necessary to take so much pains', but as they are rather obvious he would prefer to say he follows them simply because they make sense. The Conformist's reading of the Pauline formulas destroys the unique, complex unity in them which it is the original virtue of Puritanism to perceive.

III

SEPARATION

SKETCHING the manner in which dissent has developed within the Elizabethan Church, Dean John Bridges observes in 1587:

The controversies between the common adversaries [the Roman Catholics] and us are *pro Aris & focis*; for matters, & that capital matters, of the substance & life of our Christian religion. . . . Whereas the controversies betwixt us and our Brethren [the Puritans] are matters, or rather (as they call them) but manners and forms of the Church's regiment: Howbeit, whether by sufferance, or by neglect of them, grown yet unto so many heads, and so sharply prosecuted: not now contending so much for cap & surplice; nor for quarrels at the unlearneder sort of the poor ministers; nor invectives against the Bishops & their titles, or their superior jurisdictions only: but withal, calling in question all their whole authority, & their very ministry of the word and Sacraments. . . .[1]

To call into question the Bishops' 'whole authority, & their very ministry of the word and Sacraments', comes very close to suggesting that the Church of England is not a true church, for the essential marks of a true church, according to a basic dictum of the Reformation, accepted originally by Puritans and Prelates alike, are 'the preaching of the Word and the observance of the sacraments'.[2] When charged with suggesting that the Church of England is a false church, the recognized leaders of Puritanism fall back on the contention that they are only criticizing the Church's manner of using 'things indifferent'. In Cartwright's words, 'they grant that we have the church of God; but [say] that, for want of those ornaments which it should have, and through certain the deformed rags of popery which it should not have, the church doth not appear in her native colors. . . .'[3] The 'deformed rags' are literally the cap and surplice and other vestments about which the controversy began, and figuratively the Church offices upon which

---

[1] 10, Preface.
[2] 15, 1024: IV, i, 10.
[3] 120, I, 292.

it has since come to centre; and so the controversy can still be said to concern 'things indifferent' rather than the essential nature of the Church. By the same token, however, the established structure of the Church of England is seen as bearing the same relation to the 'substance & life' of the Church as the 'dead and beggarly elements' of the world to the Spirit of life.

The thought that the Church must insist on those very elements which it lives by struggling to free itself from may be called the original paradox of Conformity. It becomes difficult to maintain, however, in proportion as the idea of edification comes to be appreciated. If the Church is conceived of as a unique kind of communal order, growing by its own process of edification amid the old orders and disorders of the world, how can an institution avowedly shaped by considerations of civil order be a 'true' church? Any imposition of order from without must be seen as a denial of that living order which constitutes a church; the established structure of the Anglican Church must come to seem—in the phrase which Anthony Gilby applied to the disputed vestments—'sib the sark of *Hercules*, that made him tear his own bowels asunder'.[4] As has been seen, the reliance of the Elizabethan Church on its Reformed purity of doctrine is precisely what leads Conformists to void the word 'edification' of the meaning which Puritans find in Paul's usage of it. Thus an institution which satisfies the two Calvinist *notae ecclesiae* may nevertheless be the very antithesis of what the Puritans have come to mean by a church. Separatism springs from the original Puritan conviction that 'carnal things cannot make the perfect building of things spiritual.'[5]

'They say, the time is not yet come to build the Lord's House' cries Robert Browne in his famous 'Treatise of reformation without tarying for anie', 'they must tarry for the Magistrates and for Parliaments to do it. They want the civil sword forsooth, and the Magistrates do hinder the Lord's building and kingdom, and keep away his government.'[6] Browne's mentors, notably Cartwright, have admonished Parliaments and Prelates that ceremonies and orders contrary to the edification of the Church 'may not be established';[7] Browne simply addresses the same admonition to

---

[4] 48, Sig. K4^v.
[5] 48, Sig. H7.
[6] 13, 153.
[7] 120, II, 44.

the body of the Church itself: must it wait for the world's permission to grow? Precisely as his mentors have taught him, he argues from Pauline texts on Christian liberty that the Church may not be 'brought under the power' of the magistrate:

And this freedom have all Christians, that they consider what is lawful and what is profitable, what they may do and what is expedient [1 Cor. 6], and in no case be brought under the power of any thing, as Paul teacheth us [1 Cor. 9]. Whatsoever doth most edify, that must we choose, and avoid the contrary: and whatsoever is most expedient, that must be done, and so we must apply ourselves all unto all, that notwithstanding we hold our liberty. For if either Magistrate or other would take that from us, we must not give place by yielding unto them, no, not for an hour [Gal. 2], and this liberty is the free use of our callings and gifts, as we see most agreeing to the word of God, and expedient for his glory. Therefore the Magistrate's commandment must not be a rule unto me of this and that duty, but as I see it agree with the word of God, and expedient for his glory. . . .

The dilemma which so distressed some of Elizabeth's early bishops, whether to acquiesce in her policy with respect to indifferent things or be kept from preaching, is no problem at all once the true nature of the Church is well understood:

So then it is an abuse of my gift and calling, if I cease preaching for the Magistrate, when it is my calling to preach, yea & woe unto me, if I preach not, for necessity is laid upon me [1 Cor. 9], and if I do it unwillingly, yet the dispensation is committed unto me. And this dispensation did not the Magistrate give me, but God by consent and ratifying of the Church, and therefore as the Magistrate gave it not, so can he not take it away.[8]

The civil State is to be ordered as the civil magistrate sees fit, but the Church takes its order from the operation of God-given gifts. Cartwright condemns the architect who 'frameth his squire according to his timber and not his timber according to his squire',[9] and Browne rebukes those who, like Cartwright himself, merely try to make repairs in a building constructed so: 'The Lord's kingdom must wait on your policy forsooth, and his Church must be framed to your civil state, to supply the wants thereof: and so will ye change the Lord's government, and put your own devices in stead

[8] 13, 158–9.
[9] 17, 404.

thereof. . . .'[10] Separatists profess to respect the civil order, only
there is another kind. 'For that which we want is more than a
thousand city walls', writes Browne's associate, Robert Harrison,
'and all the cities in the world are not worth one lively church
which is God's Kingdom, wherein the throne of Christ is only
exalted, and the throne of Antichrist is laid for his footstool. And
until you see this thing brought to pass, O ye people, and see yourselves also the living stones of this living building: mourn and
lament bitterly.'[11]

'Thus the foolish Barrowist deriveth his schism by way of conclusion, as to him it seemeth, directly and plainly out of your
principles', Hooker points out to his opponents. He may be speaking better than he knows, since he appears to misconceive what the
Puritans mean by those principles of Christian liberty and edification which 'the foolish Barrowist' has taken to heart.[12] In any
case, it is enough for Hooker's purposes simply to quote the re-
proaches of the Separatist against those of his mentors, Cartwright
and Travers and the others, who still hesitate 'to erect the discipline of Christ without the leave of the Christian magistrate'.
'Him therefore,' Hooker concludes, 'we leave to be satisfied by
you from whom he hath sprung.'[13] In effect, Hooker serves notice
that the old paradoxical kind of Conformity has proved untenable.

William Perkins shows what must have been a typical response
of conservative Puritans to the choice Hooker indicates. He tacitly
—but, against the background of the vestiarian and Admonition
controversies, conspicuously—confines his expositions of Christian
liberty and edification to matters of personal morality. 'Edification', he says in *A Golden Chain*, 'is every particular duty towards
our brethren, whereby they are furthered either to grow up in

[10] 13, 167.

[11] 13, 85.

[12] 'These Officers, though they be divers and several, yet are they not
severed, lest there should be a division in the body, but they are as members of
the body, having the same care one of another, jointly doing their several duties
to the service of the Saints, and to the edification of the Body of Christ, till we
all meet together in the perfect measure of the fulness of Christ, by whom all
the body being in the meanwhile thus coupled and knit together by every joint
for the furniture thereof, according to the effectual power which is in the
measure of every part, receiveth increase of the body, unto the edifying of itself
in love. Neither can any of these Officers be wanting, without grievous lameness,
and apparent deformity of the body, yea violent injury to the Head, Christ
Jesus' (Barrow (6, 5–6)).

[13] 57, I, 117: *Laws*, Preface, viii, 1.

Christ, or else are more surely united to him (Rom. 14:19). *Let us follow those things which concern peace, and wherewith one may edify another.*' Perhaps this very text is to be understood as explaining why there is nothing about idolothytes in the list of applications which follows:

To Edification, these things which follow appertain.

I. To give good example. Matth. 5. 16. *Let your light so shine before men, that they may see your good works and glorify your Father which is in heaven.* I. Pet. 2. 12. *Have your conversation honest among the Gentiles, that they which speak evil of you as of evil doers, may by your good works which they shall see, glorify God in the day of thy visitation.*

II. To exhort. Heb. 3. 13. *Exhort one another daily, while it is called today, lest any of you be hardened through the deceitfulness of sin.* Rom. 1.12. *That I might be comforted together with you through our mutual faith, both yours & mine.*

III. To comfort. I Thess. 5.14. *Comfort the feeble minded, bear with the weak: be patient towards all men.* Jam. 5.16. *Acknowledge your faults one to another, and pray for another, that ye may be healed.* 20. *He that converteth a sinner from going astray out of his way, shall save a soul from death, and shall hide a multitude of sins.* I. Thess. 4.18. *Comfort yourselves one another, with these words.*

IV. To admonish. Rom. 15.14. *I myself am persuaded of you, brethren, that ye also are full of goodness, and filled with all knowledge: and are able to admonish one another.* I Thess. 5.14. *We desire you, brethren, admonish them that are unruly.*[14]

The familiar texts are conspicuous by their absence, and in none of those which Perkins lists does 'edification' or the verb 'to edify' appear; none is taken from a context which centres on the idea of edification. Even more striking in such a mighty man in scriptures as Perkins, the first thing to which edification is said to appertain here is a subject to which, in Paul's usage, it pertains only indirectly if at all, the effect which the behaviour of Christians is intended to have on those outside the body of Christ. Perkins is unmistakably fighting shy of the principal texts on edification and liberty. Where he does enter on one of them, in another connection, he seems aware of treading *per ignes suppositos cineri doloso*:

Good conscience is that which rightly according to God's word ex- cuseth and comforteth. For the excellency, goodness, and dignity of conscience stands not in accusing, but in excusing. And by doing any

[14] 88, 140–1.

sin whatsoever to give an occasion to the conscience to accuse and condemn, is to wound it and to offend it. Thus Paul saith that the Corinthians wounded the consciences of their weak brethren, when they used their liberty as an occasion of offence to them, I. Cor. 8,9,12.[15]

Perkins deftly plucks what he needs out of this text, the meaning of 'offence' to conscience, and because he is speaking of sins, not of things indifferent in themselves, the rest of the complex of ideas in 1 Corinthians 8 is safely irrelevant. On occasion, Perkins does take a stand on the old question of the relationship between Christian liberty and the magistrate's authority, and it is an expressly Conformist one: 'For howsoever things indifferent, after the law is once made of them, remain still indifferent in themselves, yet obedience to the law is necessary, and that for conscience sake.'[16] But apparently he avoids offending Puritan susceptibilities, his own perhaps included, by observing a 'principle of disjunction'[17] with respect to the idea of edification: he expounds it by means of texts which do not principally concern it, and when he uses a text that does contain the idea of edification in its original force and complexity, it is to expound something else.

If Perkins reconciled himself to the Conformist idea of order by quietly performing a disjunction of thought on the sore topics of Christian liberty and edification, many others probably did much the same. Such Puritans might still argue, following Bucer and Calvin, that a certain Church polity could be deduced from scripture, and wish that it might be established in England, but failing the original Puritan vision, that persuasion would become pedantic. The vision of the living Church, planted and visible in England, passes to the Separatists and to those who come to be called Congregationalists or Independents.

Their call for a 'lively Church' does not require perfection, any more than the individual Christian can presume to perfection in this life; what is looked for, both in the Church and in the individual, is the ceaseless manifestation of the Spirit of life working to

[15] 88, 867.
[16] 88, 871.
[17] The phrase is used by way of analogy with the principle set forth by Erwin Panofsky that 'classical themes transmitted to mediaeval artists by texts were anachronistically modernized' in the artists' illustrations, while 'classical images known to mediaeval artists by visual experience do not retain their original meaning but are subjected to an *interpretatio Christiana* . . .' (*Renaissance and Renascences in Western Art* (Stockholm, 1960), p. 87).

overcome whatever is not life. To the Church, therefore, disci-
plinary procedures are what repentance and the effort to keep
God's commandments are to each single member, an outward
sign—not infallible, but indispensable—of the Spirit of life within.
This is the meaning of the Separatist fervour about the 'discipline' of the Church, as Browne explains:

> Not that we can keep his commandments without all breach or offence,
> for we are not Donatists as the adversaries slander us: that we should
> say, we may be without sin, or that the church may be without public
> offences, or if there fall out some sort of grosser sins, that therefore it
> should cease to be the church of God. We teach no such doctrine, but
> if in any Church such gross sins be incurable, and the Church hath not
> power to redress them, or rebelliously refuseth to redress them, then it
> ceaseth to be the Church of God, and so remaineth till it repent & take
> better order.[18]

This is why the two Calvinist *notae ecclesiae* are insufficient; for
'neither the word in the preacher's mouth, nor the Sacraments can
make an outward Church, except they have the power of Christ to
separate the unworthy'.[19]

'The power of Christ' in the Church is what is insisted on. The
separation of the unworthy is valued as manifesting that power, and
not, as is sometimes imagined, because Separatists thought that the
presence of anyone in their midst of whose election in the secret
counsel of God there was any reason to doubt 'would infect and
corrupt all the rest'.[20] Separatist and Congregationalist spokesmen
from Browne onward acknowledge that 'there must needs be hypocrites in every church, & sometimes also open breach of God's
commandments'.[21] Not the absence of such carnal elements from
the communal body, but the evident tendency of life to transform
them or cast them off is the Separatist criterion of a true Church.
Conversely, 'where discipline is wanting, there may be some
graces of God appearing, as knowledge, and an outward subjection
to men's laws and to Magistrates, yea there may be God's secret
elect children, and an outward false show of religion and devotion:
and yet no true show nor face of an outward and visible Church of
God.'[22]

[18] 13, 459–60.
[19] 13, 443.
[20] 73, 56.
[21] 13, 441.
[22] 13, 471.

Nor is it sufficient that the unworthy should be effectively
screened out by whatever means, as it would be if the motive of
this discipline were fear of 'infection'. The means must be such as
to show the power of Christ throughout the body of the Church.
The power of binding and loosing 'is not peculiar to some one, or
to some few alone, but it belongeth to all . . .'.[23] Even supposing
an Anglican minister to be as conscientious in this matter as
George Herbert's ideal Country Parson, his church would still be
without discipline as the Separatists understand it. Moreover, the
Anglican minister's ultimate recourse must be, as Herbert says, 'to
call in Authority',[24] belying the intrinsic power of a true church to
maintain the life within it. The most rigorous administration of
this kind of discipline, however effective it might be in keeping a
congregation pure, would only confirm the Separatists' objection
that 'in the Churches of these ministers they have not this authority, but they must fetch it from otherwise, namely from their
chapital Courts: therefore they have not the Church of Christ'.[25]
It is not spiritual squeamishness, then, or a simple, 'puritanical'
moral earnestness that makes Separatists insist on 'the power of
Christ to separate the unworthy', but the conviction that 'without
the discipline and government of Christ therein, [the Church]
loseth even her essence, life & being in Christ'.[26] The Separatist
idea of discipline is a corollary of the Puritan idea of edification:
'. . . through want of discipline, there is no natural conjunction of
the parts and members of the church together, so that both the
head and vital parts are wanting, and all the other parts are wholly
and thoroughly either displaced and perverted, or utterly lost and
perished.'[27]

As a visible expression of the Church's 'life & being in Christ'
Church discipline is for the Separatist a form of communal 'confession of faith'; for as Browne says, characteristically applying to
the Church collectively a precept originally addressed to the individual believer, '. . . *Paul joineth the belief of the heart and confession
of the mouth both together, as needful unto righteousness & salvation*
[Rom. 10:10]: and by the confession of the mouth, he meaneth all

[23] 13, 443.
[24] 54, 263.
[25] 13, 32.
[26] 13, 462.
[27] 13, 463.

outward profession agreeing to faith, because the profession by mouth is chiefest.'[28] Thus all the ways in which a true Church incessantly manifests the Spirit can be comprised in terms referring properly to 'profession by mouth'; the life of the Church invites description in the familiar Old Testament terminology of the making, keeping, and renewing of covenants. From Paul's words on the necessity of outward profession, Browne goes on to assert that '. . . if among many good livers, one wicked man were found, as a murderer, an idolater, or an adulterer, and the rest become so negligent or willful, or are held in such spiritual bondage, that any one such open and manifest offence is incurable, then the covenant is broken and disanulled with them all, till they repent and redress such wickedness.' To say that the visible Church is formed by its members' adhering to a Covenant is a way of saying that 'the spirit & truth being showed by the outward good profession declare the outward Church of God, and not the places, neither temples, nor cities, not parishes'[29]—not, in short, conformity to any worldly structure.

Such, then, is the genesis of the idea of the covenanted Church out of the original Puritan protest against an ecclesiastic order sustained by 'carnal, beggarly, antichristian pomps, rites, laws, garments, and tradition'.[30] It is not as a legal contract but as a public profession of the faith that the Covenant comes to figure as the rock on which the Church is founded, as John Cotton makes especially clear:

For *Peter* himself received not the Keys merely as a Believer, but as a Believer publicly professing his faith before Christ and his fellow Disciples in Christ's School. If other Writers speak otherwise (that the Keys were given to *Peter* as a Believer in the name of Believers) they must be understood to speak of Believers, not as keeping their Faith to themselves, but as making profession of their Faith publicly, so as they come to be received into the society of the visible Church. Faith giveth a man fellowship in the Invisible Church, and in all the inward spiritual blessings of the Church, but it is profession of Faith that giveth a man fellowship in the visible Church. It is not a society of Believers, as such, that maketh them a Church; for a society of Christian Merchants may meet together in a ship to transport themselves to Hamburg or Lubeck, but they are not thereby a Church, nor have received Church-power.

[28] 13, 438.
[29] 13, 448.
[30] 48, Sig. C5^v.

But if they do publicly profess their Faith, and their obedience of Faith to the Lord Jesus in the public ordinances of his worship, which he hath committed to his Church, and they are capable of; then indeed they are a professed visible Church of Christ, and a Body united to him, and to one another by such profession. . . .[31]

Being well suited to concise, legalistic formulation, the idea of the Covenant becomes especially conspicuous in formal Church platforms, but in the polemical documents of Separatism and Congregationalism it takes its place in the complex of ideas and expressions which originally crystallized in the vestiarian controversy.

That the Church Covenant is conceived of primarily as a manifestation of the new life of the Spirit is evident not only from the way the idea first appears among the Separatists, but also from the manner of taking the Covenant which develops later among Congregationalists. Congregational Churches in the seventeenth century are less interested in doctrinal knowledgeability than in 'taking notice of the least breathings of Christ, in those that offer themselves to join with them in Church communion . . .'.[32] If the 'least breathings' of life in Christ are there, edification will follow. Thus the original principles of Puritanism lead to a special kind of 'internal toleration', as it may be called, based not on scepticism about the possibility of sure knowledge, but on the conviction that where 'the root of the matter' is in a man, that which is lacking in his faith will grow to perfection within the Church:

Those of the Congregational way, are content to receive such into communion and church fellowship, upon their proffering themselves, that differ from them in their judgement, in things of lesser consequence and moment, so long as they have good evidence and testimony of their upright conversation, and find them willing to sit down with them, and submit themselves to the church's proceedings, as far as God shall give them light.

The doctrinal aspect of the Covenant can therefore be reduced to elementary essentials; and since the 'testimony of upright conversation' of people seeking Church fellowship is unlikely to present much difficulty or interest, the outward profession of

[31] 28, 39–40.

[32] This and the two following quotations are from William Bartlet, 'Ιχνογραφία, or a Model of The Primitive Congregational Way (1647), as quoted by Geoffrey F. Nuttall (81, 109–10).

people entering the Church tends to resolve itself into a testimony of spiritual experience. 'Those of the Congregational way' are eager to recognize

... the meanest work of grace, where they have any the least hints of truth and sincerity, being assured that Christ hath appointed his green Pastures for his weak Lambs, as well as for his grown sheep.

They are willing to give liberty to any such poor souls to manifest what God hath done for them in uniting them to Christ the foundation ... for the satisfying of those that shall have communion with them in the holy things of God, ... either before the whole Church publicly, or else if they are weak and bashful (as many are) to the Pastor in private, with one or two more of the Church, and they to transmit it to the Church.

There is no evidence that anyone who made such profession of his spiritual experience was ever refused church membership simply because his 'relation' failed to convince the congregation that he meant it.[33] The mere fact of being expected to make an open profession of this kind would undoubtedly deter many people and

[33] Edmund S. Morgan (77, 93–9) shows that in all probability the practice of calling on new members to give testimony of their spiritual experience first arose as a part of the general 'prophesying' which Congregationalists set such store by. Doubtless it always appeared in this light to most of the participants. The criterion for a proper narrative of conversion experience according to Thomas Shepard is that it should consist only of such things 'as may be of special use unto the people of God' (quoted by Morgan, p. 92). Morgan's thesis, however, leads him to play down this positive aspect of the practice, and to treat it as a more and more rigorous 'test', conducted in a spirit of jealous exclusivism. Yet he cannot adduce a single reported instance of a candidate's failing simply because his narrative seemed inadequate. He appears to regard as such an instance the refusal of a committee of New England ministers to approve a proposed new church at Dorchester in 1636 because, as Winthrop reports, the men who proposed to found it were unable to 'manifest the work of God's grace in themselves'. The grounds which Winthrop cites are:

1. That they had not come to hate sin, because it was filthy, but only left it, because it was hurtful. 2. That, by reason of this, they had never truly closed with Christ, (or rather Christ with them,) but had made use of him only to help the imperfection of their sanctification and duties, and not made him their sanctification, wisdom, etc. 3. They expected to believe by some power of their own, and not only and wholly from Christ.

'In other words,' Morgan concludes, 'the proposed founders of the Dorchester church were insufficiently familiar with the morphology of conversion and so had deceived themselves' (pp. 100–1). It would be more exact to say that these overt doctrinal errors meant that these people did not strictly profess to be founding their church on 'the work of God's grace in themselves'. The very fact that the narratives of spiritual experience are stereotyped according to the doctrinal scheme which Morgan aptly terms 'the morphology of conversion'

thereby function as an effectual test, but it would do so, not on the basis of any 'infatuated notion that the church can discern between regeneration and reprobation',[34] but simply on the principle that 'all that truly believe, profess; though all that profess, do not truly believe'.[35]

The Congregational Church Covenant has sometimes been said to express a principle of 'voluntarism'.[36] This description contains an important element of truth, but outside the context of ideas in which the idea of the Church Covenant arose it is likely to be seriously misleading. Its truth lies in the fact that Separatists and Congregationalists do insist that the power of Christ which forms a church works in mysterious conjunction with the will of man. The visible Church, William Ames says,

differs from the mystical Church, the gathering of which together into one is not prescribed unto men, but performed immediately by divine operation, but the gathering together into an instituted Church is so performed by God, that his command and man's duty and labour do come between.[37]

However, Ames immediately adds, the Church

is ordained by God and Christ only, because men have neither power of themselves to institute, or frame a Church unto Christ, neither have they by the revealed will of God any such power committed to them: their greatest honor is that they are servants in the House of God. *Heb.* 3.5.

He does not say that the churches men establish by voluntary association must meet the requirements of a revealed 'constitution'; he says men have no power of themselves to form churches. In fact, he does not go into ecclesiastic polity or the marks of a true Church, finding it sufficient to say that a Church is formed when believers are 'joined together by a special bond among themselves':

This bond is a covenant, either express or implicit, whereby believers do particularly bind themselves to perform all those duties, both to-

shows that the only aspect of them which could be called a 'test' was doctrinal. The only kind of 'sincerity' it can have been thought of as ascertaining was orthodoxy concerning such matters as the connection between mortification for sins and regeneration, and the relation of grace to human efforts.

[34] 71, 88.
[35] John Owen, *Of Schisme*, quoted by Nuttall (81, 67).
[36] 81, 106 ff.
[37] 2, 141–2.

ward God and one toward another, which pertain to the respect and edification of the Church.

This last phrase, when fully understood, indicates what the Congregationalist means by saying that a church is 'ordained by God and Christ only': only as it looks toward the edification of that unique communal order which is the body of Christ can a covenant among men be called a Church:

This joining together by covenant doth only so far forth make a Church as it respects the exercising the communion of Saints: for the same believing men may join themselves in covenant to make a City or some civil society, as they do immediately respect a common civil good, but they do not make a Church but as in their constitution they respect holy communion with GOD among themselves.

Hence the same men may make a City or politic society and not a Church; or a Church, and not a City; or both a Church and a City.

. . . Neither yet doth some sudden joining together and exercise of holy communion suffice to make a Church, unless there be also that constancy, at least in intention, which brings the state of a body, and members in a certain spiritual polity.[38]

This 'exercising the communion of saints' is to be understood as a constant intercommunication of the Spirit among the members. Were it not so, one of the distinguishing features of Congregationalism, its refusal to extend the title of 'Church' beyond a single, fairly small gathering of people, would be simply unaccountable. There is nothing to prevent men from voluntarily committing themselves to larger associations such as—to take the principal case in point—the Presbyterian synods. Ames observes that 'the light of nature and equity of rules and examples of Scripture' amply warrant a more extensive 'mutual confederacy' than that of a particular congregation, yet he insists that such a 'combination doth neither constitute a new form of a Church, neither ought it to take away, or diminish any way, that liberty and power which Christ hath left to his Churches . . .'.[39] When he speaks of 'that liberty and power which Christ hath left to his Churches', Ames is thinking of one of the favourite Puritan texts:

But unto every one of us is given grace according to the measure of the gift of Christ. Wherefore he saith, When he ascended up on high, he

[38] 2, 142.
[39] 2, 179.

led captivity captive, and gave gifts unto men. . . . And he gave some, apostles; and some, prophets; and some, evangelists; and some, pastors and teachers; For the perfecting of the saints, for the work of the ministry, for the edifying of the body of Christ (Eph. 4:7–8, 11–12).

This process can hardly take place among *disjecta membra*. Strangers meeting on the road may fall into 'good discourses, such as may edify', as Herbert's Country Parson is careful to do where-ever he goes,[40] but in the full sense which it has had from the beginning in Puritan accounts of the nature of the Church, 'edification' among members who rarely or never meet is a contradiction in terms. Thus the limitation of the form of a visible Church to a single congregation is a palpable consequence of the conviction that true Church order is not created by the will of men but by the power of Christ, 'From whom the whole body fitly joined together and compacted by that which every joint supplieth, according to the effectual working in the measure of every part, maketh increase of the body unto the edifying of itself in love' (Eph. 4:16).

If a single phrase had to be chosen to summarize everything that Separatists and Congregationalists abhor, it might be 'voluntary Religions'.[41] No act 'grounded only upon the will of man, and not upon the word of God . . . can be an act of Religion', says William Bradshaw; to ascribe religious value to any such merely voluntary act is to make it an act 'of superstition'.[42] By insisting that the act of consent whereby believers form a church is voluntary, Separatists do not mean that a church is created by the concurrence of sovereign wills; they mean that a living temple can only be built of living stones. When Ames notes the similarity between the Church Covenant and those covenants by which 'the same believing men may join themselves to make a City or some civil society', it is in order to define the difference. Civil societies originate properly and necessarily by the will of man; that is what is meant by calling civil policy 'carnal'. Where such policy is directed by believers, it is to be used to foster the Church. Christian magistrates are called upon, in the curious biblical phrase, to be 'nursing fathers' to the Church (Isa. 49:23)—hence the 'theocracy' of early New England —, but the only religious sanction enjoyed by any civil bond among men is based precisely on the recognition that it is no part

[40] 54, 251.
[41] 117, 71.
[42] 9, 23.

of 'Christ's kingdom': 'As Christ's kingdom is not of this world [John 18:36], so neither doth it destroy or abolish the policies of the same, but maintain them rather, while it teacheth all men to do their duty, and subject themselves, even for conscience' sake [Rom. 13:5; Eccles. 10:20].'[43]

So much could be said with reference to a thoroughly heathen State or a 'secular city', should the Church find itself in the midst of one. Indeed, the Church would be better off in such circumstances than in a Christian State which pretended to sanctify 'policy':

> For we know that when Magistrates have been most of all against the Church and the authority thereof, the Church hath most flourished. Woe to you therefore ye blind Preachers and hypocrites, for ye spread a veil of darkness upon the people, and bring upon them a cursed covering, because by your policy you hide them under the power of Antichrist, and keep from their eyes the kingdom of Christ.[44]

Seventeenth-century Separatists and Congregationalists assume that civil society is formed by voluntary compacts among men, but that is not their distinctive contribution to later-day democracy. Their distinctive contribution can only be their insistence that civil order of any kind, precisely because it is created by human will, has no claim to worship. If, as R. H. Tawney says, medieval thought tends to ascribe to social institutions 'a character which may almost be called sacramental',[45] then it is true that the strain of Puritanism which is being followed here destroys that happy synthesis of politics and religion. Where medieval thought defends the social hierarchy by the analogy of the human body,[46] Puritan thought distinguishes between the order that is created by life in the body of Christ and that order which is constructed out of the wills, appetites, and 'imaginations' of men. Civil order is to be respected and can be made to reflect, partially and provisionally, the order of Christ's kingdom, but to confuse it with the kind of order which can only appear in a visible Church is to 'spread a veil of darkness upon the people . . . and keep from their eyes the kingdom of Christ'.

Paradoxically, however, once the Puritan conception of the

---

[43] I, 347–8.
[44] 13, 167.
[45] III, 21.
[46] III, 22 ff.

Church has been put in terms of the Church Covenant, the possibility of a new compromise with the Established Church appears. Where a congregation covenants to form a church and circumstances conspire to let them have a minister appointed over them who is also in Covenant with them, what essential difference does it make if they occupy the place of a parish? A congregation which enters into a Covenant expressing 'that liberty and power which Christ hath left to his Churches' will surely know how to regard the cope and surplice. In effect, their Covenant can function instead of those constant explanations of Christian liberty by which Anglican ministers in the early days were supposed to obviate the dangers of the vestments they wore. The covenanted Church can be an *ecclesiola in ecclesia*, or more precisely, a true Church as judged by its manifestation of the power of Christ within a true Church as judged by its purity of doctrine. If the congregation 'tarries' thus within the old edifice of policy, it is to avoid the 'offence' of outright separation from their weaker brethren. It appears that such an arrangement was widely adopted in seventeenth-century England.[47]

This compromise means that covenanted congregations recognize other congregations of the Church of England as true Churches, even those which have not drawn up a Church Covenant among themselves. To do so, however, might seem to be an admission that Cartwright was right after all when he told Harrison that 'the discipline' was not really necessary to the very being of the Church, but only to its 'comeliness' and 'long continuance':

And first of all to the reason of the discipline, for the want whereof you give them all [that is, the parish churches] without exception the black stone of condemnation from being the churches of Christ . . . it is to be understood that as in a man there are certain parts essential and such as without which the man cannot stand, and other some serving either to his comeliness or to his long continuance, so it is in this matter: there is the foundation, Christ, whereupon it is necessary that by faith the assemblies be laid, which groweth unto the Lord's building, without the which it cannot be his church; which thing being [that is, so long as faith exists in the church] whatsoever is either wanting of that which is commanded, or remaining of that which is forbidden, is not able to put that assembly which by faith is laid upon Christ from the right and title of being the church of Christ. . . .[48]

47 81, 9–14, 22 ff., 134 ff.   48 16, 53.

In spite of all he had told Whitgift about 'offence' and 'shipwreck of conscience', Cartwright still believed that doctrinal faith was enough to assure that a parish church would grow into 'the Lord's building'. But his pupil Browne had retorted, still in the language of 'edification', that

... if we shall live by faith, then faith is the means to come by life, and is not the life itself. Wherefore Christ is the life and essence of the Church, and not faith. Now Christ is made as no christ unto us, except we hold him, and join with him as our annointed King, priest and Prophet. ... And here I demand of M. C. whether the Kingdom, Priesthood, & Prophecy of Christ be of the essence and life of the Church. I am sure he dare not say nay to this: and why then will he have the Lord's discipline or government to be but an accident or hang-by to the church? *For by Christ*, as Paul showeth, (*that is by the graces of Christ's kingdom, priesthood, & prophecy*) *all his body*, (*that is all his Church*) *are coupled & knit together by every joint, and so receiveth increase and edifying in God.* So take away the kingdom and government of Christ, and there can be no joining, nor coupling together of the church, no offices nor callings in the Church, yea, no face, or show, or rather no part, sign or token of the church.[49]

The choice between taking the idea of edification seriously or only mystically, so to speak, seemed clear and compelling. 'Indeed it is true', Browne wrote, 'that we ought jointly to execute this power', and so avoid Separation if possible; 'but if others will not or be in bondage that they cannot join with us therein, then they are not the Church, but the bondslaves of men.'[50] And yet the 'semi-separatists', as they are called,[51] must extend to whole congregations which 'will not or be in bondage that they cannot' join in Covenants the 'right and title to being the Church of Christ'.

The argument by which it is proposed to solve this difficulty is epitomized in Ames' carefully modified definition of a Church Covenant as 'a covenant, either express or implicit . . .'. In order not to declare that most of the parish churches in England are false, it is necessary to give them all the benefit of a doubt which they themselves hardly entertain. Whether they know it or not, they have all particularly bound themselves in an 'implicit' Covenant.

The nature of this compromise has been misrepresented in after

[49] 13, 462.
[50] 13, 443–4.
[51] 81, 10.

times because of a modern *idée fixe* concerning the place of the doctrine of predestination in radical Protestantism. Although Browne scarcely alludes to predestination, and then only in order to make clear that 'there may be God's secret elect children' outside the Church and hypocrites within it, Perry Miller explains that Browne's starting point was the conviction that 'a church of the elect existing within a church of the doomed was an anomalous arrangement'.[52] Separatist polity, Miller says, 'intended in the first place to interpret predestination literally. Only persons who could prove that they were "redeemed by Christ vnto holiness & happiness for euer" could be church members, and they could not afford to admit into the fellowship any of the wicked and ungodly, for to do so would infect and corrupt all the rest.'[53] Although they

[52] 73, 55. Miller goes on to say of Browne, 'Whether or not he was influenced by continental Anabaptism remains a moot question, but there is no doubt he himself thought he had found his inspiration in the revealed Word.' Since Browne is well known to have been influenced by Cartwright, since his declarations clearly resemble those which Puritans had been making for years, and since he differs from the Anabaptists on the point of infant baptism, it seems uninstructive to go on mooting the question whether he was influenced by Anabaptism particularly. In any case, similarities between Separatist polity and that of Continental Anabaptists might well suggest the opposite of what Miller supposes about the bearing of the doctrine of predestination on that polity. Jacques Courvoisier observes, speaking of Bucer's reply to the challenge of the Anabaptists: 'La doctrine de la prédestination le plaçait sur un terrain où il était inexpugnable, car à la communauté des saints dont parlaient les Anabaptistes il opposait toujours la communauté des élus. Or si l'on peut voir qui est saint, puisqu'on connait l'arbre à son fruit, on ne peut jamais savoir exactement qui est élu. Et cela justifie l'Église populaire, multitudiniste, qui seule assure l'instruction religieuse de tous, donc seule peut être en mesure de manifester le decret de Dieu' (29, 78). To be sure, Miller asserts that the English Separatists and Congregationalists did think they could tell 'exactement qui est élu', but in fact they only claimed to discern 'saints' by outward profession.

[53] 73, 55–6. The phrase which Miller quotes from Browne here occurs in a brief description of the Church in which observations such as Browne makes elsewhere about the presence of hypocrites in it would be out of place. To say that 'Christians are a company of believers, which by a willing covenant made with their God, are under the government of God and Christ . . . Because they are redeemed by Christ' is only to indicate what people profess who enter into Covenant; Browne says nothing about their having to 'prove' it. Edmund S. Morgan points out that Browne nowhere describes 'any effort by the church to search the religious experiences of the members' (77, 38). Morgan shows that 'in all probability no such test was applied by the Separatist churches in Holland or by the Plymouth church in the 1620's' (p. 65). However, while correcting Miller's factual assertions on this point, Morgan retains the preconceived idea of the Separatists' basic motive which those factual assertions were made to support: 'The Separatists withdrew from the Church of England in order to

never say anything of the sort, Miller can tell that these exaltedly self-complacent people mean nothing less than to anticipate the Last Judgement:

Though God alone knew whom He had chosen, still if the churches rigorously examined their candidates and kept a close watch over their members, they might be practically certain that those who took the church covenant had also been received into the covenant of grace with God himself. The visible Church would thus become a genuine preparatory school for the invisible, and the covenanted brethren could make in it the acquaintance of their future neighbors in heaven.[54]

On this assumption, the semi-separatist compromise must indeed appear ridiculous. If a merely implicit entrance examination is a sufficient gesture toward the 'restriction of church membership to the proved elect',[55] what meaning is left in 'proved'? It might be expected that the 'superlative genius for casuistry'[56] which Miller attributes to non-separating Congregationalists would be much occupied on this point, and likewise that their critics among the stricter Separatists would have many quotable things to say about

establish churches of their own in which the membership would more closely approximate that of the invisible church. . . . They therefore set up standards of membership by which to control both the admission of members and their continuance in the church' (pp. 33–4). If this was their idea of what they were doing, their failure to include anything beyond 'historical' faith and outward conduct in their 'standards' is hard to explain. Morgan can only account for it by supposing, in effect, that they simply had not given sufficient thought to these matters to perceive how inconsistent their plan for approximating the invisible Church was with the most elementary principles of their own theology:

The faith implied in a confession of faith was not saving faith but simply an intellectual understanding of, and consent to, a set of doctrines; it was the product, not of grace but of instruction. To distinguish such faith from saving faith, Puritans often called it 'general' or 'historical' faith. Saving faith must be preceded by historical faith, but historical faith was not necessarily followed by saving faith. Separatists doubtless assumed that a probability of salvation attended those who possessed historical faith and also obeyed God's commandments outwardly (p. 43).

They need not have assumed anything of the sort, however, if their motives for Separation were what they said they were. Separatists and Congregationalists never say that they are trying to make the membership of the visible Church coincide as closely as possible with that of the invisible, whereas they do continually affirm that a true church must manifest the Spirit of life in its profession and discipline. Presumably such a 'lively' church will also correspond to the invisible Church more closely than a false church does, but that is not the consideration that apologists for the polity concern themselves with.

[54] 73, 57.
[55] 73, 77.
[56] 73, 84.

the difference between this implicit examination and the rigorous proof they themselves exacted of candidates. Yet in all his entertaining reconstruction of the 'cobweb of sophistry'[57] that the non-separating brethren wove and the 'puzzled' rejoinders of the honest Separatists, the nearest thing to an argument on this supposedly essential feature of polity that Miller can quote is a remark by Ames that 'from a fundamentally true church "in which some wicked men are tollerated, we must not presently separate"'.[58] A Separatist would say indeed we must 'presently separate', but to neither party would 'wicked men' be equivalent to 'the non-elect'; Ames is replying to assertions like Browne's that 'open and gross sinners shall not be suffered in the Church'.[59] Conversely, neither Separatists nor semi-separatists ever speak of the visible Church as a gathering of the elect; it is 'gathered of the worthy'.[60] Who these are is explained by Cotton, defending an argument for Congregationalism based on the interpretation of the Temple in Jerusalem as a type of the visible Church: 'There were no stones at all in the Temple of Jerusalem, but choice, and well-squared stones' one challenging objection ran—'are there no Members of the visible Church, but chosen of God?' Cotton replies:

We do not say that there are no members of the visible Church but the chosen of God; but this we say, that none should be laid in the Fellowship of the Church, who are but sandy and miry Professors, and hold forth no solid firmness of a Christian profession. Though we cannot easily judge, who are the chosen ones of God in his eternal counsel; yet we may discern a difference between precious and vile, as *Solomon's* builders did discern a difference between Free stones and the common Pebbles of the streets; and as bulchy swellings of stones in the quarry had need to be hewn and squared that they may lie level with other stones in the building, and suit the proportion of the house, so we conceive natural and carnal worldings and malignants opposite to grace and truth had need to be hewn and planed by the Ministry of the word, that they may lie level to the Ordinances of God and to the fellowship of their Brethren when they come to be laid together in the Church-building. And such as are so prepared may be accounted choice persons in comparison of many others.[61]

---

[57] With his quite unsubstantiated representation of this 'cobweb of sophistry' Miller begins his vindication of 'the majesty and coherence of Puritan thinking' (73, xx).

[58] 73, 87; quoting (in double quotation marks here) Ames, *Conscience*, p. 62.

[59] 13, 459.   [60] 13, 464.   [61] 27, 85–6.

Neither Separatists nor nonseparating Congregationalists ever dreamed of basing Church membership on election in the secret counsel of God. That not all the 'worthy' are finally chosen is a mystery they do not meddle with.[62]

The semi-separatist position, then, is not so patently absurd, or indeed dishonest, as it has been made to appear. It does not require saving appearances for 'a church of the elect existing within a church of the doomed', but only a charitable acknowledgment of 'the least breathings of Christ' in the weaker congregations of the English Church. If the substantial intention of a Covenant, by virtue of which it forms a living church, is 'outward good profession', it is not unreasonable to argue that in any regular assembly of good Christians for worship

There wants not that reall and substantiall comming together, (or agreeing in Covenant, though more implicate then were meete) and that substantiall profession of Faith, which (thanks be to God) hath preserved the essence of visible Churches in *England* unto this day.[63]

This is an avowedly uneasy compromise, but in relation to the real nature and original understanding of the Separatist Church Covenant it is defensible in good faith. By it covenanted congregations are enabled to go on in their way, realizing in practice the idea of a visible Church which sixteenth-century Puritans found in the Epistles of Paul, the idea of a unique communal order, 'an Organical Political body', as it comes to be called,[64] edified by the Spirit of new life in its members. Far from being based on a 'stark Biblical literalism' such as is sometimes imagined to represent 'the spirit of primitive Protestantism',[65] this Puritan conception develops out of a lively and penetrating study of the work of one of the most powerful minds of antiquity. It is only to be expected that such a conception would often be misapprehended, distorted, or simply forgotten in the turbulent course of the seventeenth century. Where it was not understood or ceased to be well understood,

---

[62] Compare Hooker, 57, II, 311: *Laws*, V, lxiv, 2: 'In sum, the whole Church is a multitude of believers, all honoured with that title, even hypocrites for their profession's sake as well as saints because of their inward sincere persuasion. . . .' The only point on which Separatists would quarrel with this statement is the implied extensiveness of the 'multitude' which can constitute a visible church.

[63] Robert Parker, quoted in Richard Mather, *An Apologie of the Churches in New England* (1643), p. 36; here quoted from Miller (73, 87).

[64] John Owen, *Of Schisme*, quoted by Nuttall (81, 68).

[65] 71, 250.

Puritan insistence that Church polity should be 'grounded of the word of God' might easily seem, or insensibly degenerate into, an uninspired and uncritical legalism. What is remarkable, however, is that the Pauline conception of the living Church evidently did come to be appropriated, without losing its essential features and force, by great numbers of 'simple-minded but sincere and sensitive' people.[66]

[66] 81, 45.

IV

FROM GENERATION TO GENERATION

THE Puritan theme of edification represents the element of Paul's theology of the Church which has its source, as L. Cerfaux has said, in 'the Christian experience' itself.[1] As the individual convert to Christ is 'baptized into his death' and born into a new kind of life 'in the likeness of his resurrection', so the whole company of Christians participates in a new kind of communal life as the body of Christ.

Neither for the Church collectively nor for the individual is the moment of Christ's coming the end of the story; for each it is the beginning of a new process of growth in this world. Thus Paul's conception of the mystery of death and rebirth in Christ differs radically from mystic religions of a simply Hellenic kind, for which the experience of the mystery is inconsequential and static. Even where such Hellenic mysticism has been philosophized in the Platonic manner, the mystery itself has no consequences in the temporal course of life; it is only the hope of ultimately participating in the mystery that has temporal consequences, functioning as a motive of virtue: '. . . for the sake of these things which we have described,' Socrates tells a disciple just before his own philosophic Passion, 'we should leave nothing undone to participate in virtue and understanding in this life; for the prize is noble and the expectation great (καλὸν γὰρ τὸ ἆθλον καὶ ἡ ἐλπὶς μεγάλη).'[2] Paul evokes a hope of ultimate reward in similar language, and yet the

---

[1] 18, 283: 'Thus the two-sidedness of Paul's theology of the Church is explained by its twofold revealed source: the theology of the people of God, and the Christian experience.' On this and many other points Cerfaux strikingly supports the reading of Paul's theology of the Church which the present study attempts to trace through the development of English Puritanism. Of the major aspects of Paul's thought concerning the Church which Puritanism brings out, only one, in fact, is missing from Cerfaux's account: that is, the significance of the topic of idolothytes as suggesting the difference in kind between the Church community and other forms of social organization. The fact that Cerfaux is not led into this aspect of the matter appears to corroborate the thesis that the English situation under Elizabeth produced a distinctive 'commentary' on Paul.

[2] *Phaedo* 114c.

mystery has already been accomplished for those whom he exhorts to the contest. This paradox in the individual life corresponds to the 'post-messianic' situation of the Church collectively, in which the eschatological expectations of Israel are both accomplished and yet to come. Just as the individual's conversion to Christ begins his struggle, so the historical moment of Christ by no means disengages the Church from its age. Of Paul's various metaphors, that of the continuing edification of the temple of God serves best to make comprehensible this paradox of a mystic 'end' and fulfilment, which is at the same time the beginning of a new kind of engagement in temporal experience and history. The new birth in Christ is the decisive event both for the Church collectively and for the individual, but it is not the final event: it is the beginning of growth.

However, the Pauline concept of edification encounters a difficulty as a description of the ongoing history of the Church which does not appear when it is applied to the ongoing struggle of the individual convert. It envisions only a single life span. Growth, as it is understood in Paul's thought—and in the ancient world generally—is not simply quantitative increase, which might go on indefinitely, though pointlessly; rather, edification should come to an end in 'that which is perfect' or fully matured ($\tau\grave{o}$ $\tau\acute{\epsilon}\lambda\epsilon\iota\upsilon\nu$). The child will put away childish things in due course; and the work of the ministry aims at 'the edifying of the body of Christ: Till we all come in the unity of the faith, and the knowledge of the Son of God, unto a perfect man ($\epsilon\grave{\iota}s$ $\check{\alpha}\nu\delta\rho\alpha$ $\tau\acute{\epsilon}\lambda\epsilon\iota\upsilon\nu$), unto the measure of the stature of the fulness of Christ' (Eph. 4:12–13). For the individual this final perfection can be supposed to come with the end of his earthly life span, as Paul's description of it in his discourse on faith, hope, and charity indicates; but the idea of a corresponding historic end of communal edification, if such an idea is implicit in Paul's words on the subject, must soon fade into the future along with the idea of the Second Coming. It cannot sustain an ecclesiastical institution over the centuries. Nothing in the idea of edification suggests continuity from generation to generation. On the contrary, the metaphor of growth to maturity applies properly only to a single organism in its own generation. Taken by itself the idea of edification positively militates against the historical extension of the Church beyond a single generation of converts to Christ.

This latent difficulty can be illustrated by one of the earliest documents of English Puritanism, the 'General Letter sent from the congregation of Frankfort to Strassburg, Zurich, Wezeil, Emden, etc.' during the Marian exile. Quoting Ephesians 4, the Frankfurt congregation admonishes the others that Paul there describes the Church order ordained by the Lord 'to confirm the godly and to labor to finish the building of Christ's body till we be all brought to one consent in faith, to the knowledge of the son of God, to a perfect man, and finally to the just measure of a ripe Christian age'. The important word for the present purpose is 'finish'. Wishing to exhort those who have begun reforming the Church not to stop short, the Frankfurt congregation calls attention especially to the fact that Paul describes the process of edification as continuing until its envisioned end:

Let us all mark, that he saith not that God hath left the scriptures only, that everyone should read it, but also that he hath erected a policy and order that there should be some to teach, and not for one day, but all the time of our life even to the death, for that is the time of our perfection. Wherefore, brethren, let us submit ourselves and leave off farther to tempt God, seeing that if we will be of the body of Christ we must obey to this general rule. Let no respect of worldly policy stay us.[3]

At the beginning of the passage the envisioned end of the process of 'building' is a time when the whole Church will come 'to one consent in faith . . . to the just measure of a ripe Christian age', but as soon as the actual duration of the process comes to be stressed it can only be thought of in terms of individual lives. This momentary obscuration of the communal idea passes easily enough (partly by virtue of a convenient ambiguity in the first person plural pronoun, which oscillates between referring to the collective entity whose order Paul describes and referring distributively to individuals) but it is not insignificant. Paul may well have thought of the collective edification of the Church and that of the first generation of individual believers as proceeding *pari passu* to a common point of perfection at the imminent end of the age, but those who respond to his vision fifteen centuries later cannot think of the temporal growth of the Church to perfection as coincident with the earthly life span of its present members.[4] For them the idea of edification cannot describe the temporal dimension of the Church.

[3] 122, xii.
[4] Paul probably envisioned an interval of forty years, by a familiar Old

The problem of defining the Church as a historical institution, or, more properly, of redefining its historical nature on the basis of the Bible alone, is a prominent concern of the Reformation.[5] To regard the problem in the light of the Pauline idea of the living Church is only to accentuate it; yet when English Puritans address themselves to describing the historical continuity of the Church they by no means find themselves obliged to supplement Paul. Like their Continental brethren generally, they find the idea of the historical Church in another aspect of Paul's thought, one which, happily enough, Paul himself describes in terms of a covenant.

Paul's arguments concerning Christian liberty are not always based on the believer's 'death' to sin and his new life in Christ. The very 'manifesto' of Christian liberty, in fact, the Epistle to the Galatians, presents an argument which is basically independent of 'Christ-mysticism':

> Even as Abraham believed God, and it was accounted to him for righteousness. Know ye therefore that they which are of faith, the same are the children of Abraham. And the scripture, foreseeing that God would justify the heathen through faith, preached before the gospel unto Abraham, saying, In thee shall all nations be blessed. So then they which be of faith are blessed with faithful Abraham (3:6–9).

This argument could stand by itself without reference to the mystery of participation in a death and a new birth. Paul connects it to that mystery by asserting that the 'seed' of Abraham, to which the promise was made, is Christ: 'He saith not, And to seeds, as of many; but as of one, And to thy seed, which is Christ' (3:16). This identification of the whole people with the single person of the Messiah is in accord with a well-attested tendency in the Old Testament and Judaism,[6] although Paul sees that identification in a way that is decisively new. His concept of corporate identification with Christ by participation in the mystery of his death and resurrection so transforms the Old Testament way of thinking of

Testament usage the time of one generation, between the Passion and the Parousia. See Hans-Joachim Schoeps (103, 100). Schoeps follows Albert Schweitzer (105) in emphasizing that Paul's message is directed to the unique situation of the generation living on earth during that interval.

[5] See John M. Headley, *Luther's View of Church History* (53).

[6] The name of Wheeler Robinson 'is especially associated with the idea of "corporate personality", though he was not the only one, or even the first, to draw attention to the phenomenon of thought which the term denotes. It was he who brought it into special prominence, and who applied it fruitfully to

'corporate personality' as to obscure the fact that it is still opera-tive in his thought. Nevertheless, for the specific argument for Christian liberty which he draws from the nature of the Covenant with Abraham that great transformation of the Old Testament way of conceiving collective identity is not absolutely necessary. For that argument it is enough that the story of the chosen people should be seen to begin simply with God's making a promise to Abraham and Abraham's believing God. That fact of the story in Genesis is enough to show that the ordinances in question between Paul and his Judaizing opponents cannot be essential to the special relationship between God and his chosen people and need not be required eternally. Since they were added later for certain pur-poses of God's historic dispensation, there may come a time still later when they are no longer required, and Paul argues that that time has come: 'Christ hath redeemed us from the curse of the law, being made a curse for us: for it is written, Cursed is every one that hangeth on a tree' (3:13). Christ's death on the 'tree' can be said to effect this historical change without any necessary refer-ence to the believer's mystic participation in his death and resur-rection. In the new age which that event begins in the history of the chosen people, the essential faith of Abraham, which since the time of Moses has been obscured by the Law, stands fully revealed as the *fons et origo* of God's Israel.

If the argument for Christian liberty which follows from the convert's new life in Christ tends to set the Gospel off against the Old Testament, this other equally Pauline argument from the Covenant with Abraham has the opposite tendency. To interpret Christian liberty in simple opposition to the religion of the Old Testament is thus to assert one part of the Pauline synthesis in the name of the whole. Such a separation of the New Testament from the Old was one of the most heinous offences of Servetus, accord-ing to Calvin, and it is in answer to Servetus on this point that Calvin introduces his discussion in the *Institutes* of the Pauline argument from the Covenant:

Here we must take our stand on three main points. First, we hold that carnal prosperity and happiness did not constitute the goal set before

some of the outstanding problems of the Old Testament ...' (H. H. Rowley in the Introduction to *The Old Testament and Modern Study* (98, xxix)). See par-ticularly Robinson's paper on 'The Hebrew Conception of Corporate Per-sonality' (94).

the Jews to which they were to aspire. Rather, they were adopted into
the hope of immortality; and assurance of this adoption was certified to
them by oracles, by the law, and by the prophets. Secondly, the covenant by which they were bound to the Lord was supported, not by their
own merits, but solely by the mercy of the God who called them.
Thirdly, they had and knew Christ as Mediator, through whom they
were joined to God and were to share in his promises.[7]

These points simply amplify Paul's assertion that 'the scripture
... preached before the gospel (προευηγγελίσατο) unto
Abraham'. Abraham and the other Patriarchs really believed in
the Gospel of Christ, whom they had dimly in view in the form of
ceremonial types; and the various promises made to the Jews in
material terms were chiefly intended to set forth spiritual promises
in a manner calculated to appeal immediately to childlike appre-
hensions. Here the metaphor of growth to maturity is applied on a
historical scale to help explain God's curious manner of dealing
by indirections with his chosen people:

This will be more apparent from the comparison that Paul made in the
letter to the Galatians. He compares the Jewish nation to a child heir,
not yet fit to take care of himself, under the charge of a guardian or
tutor to whose care he has been entrusted. . . . Therefore the same inheritance was appointed for them and for us, but they were not yet old
enough to be able to enter upon it and manage it. The same church
existed among them, but as yet in its childhood. Therefore, keeping
them under this tutelage, the Lord gave, not spiritual promises un-
adorned and open, but ones foreshadowed, in a measure, by earthly
promises. When, therefore, he adopted Abraham, Isaac, Jacob, and
their descendants into the hope of immortality, he promised them the
Land of Canaan as an inheritance. It was not to be the final goal of their
hopes, but was to exercise and confirm them, as they contemplated it,
in hope of their true inheritance, an inheritance not yet manifested to
them.[8]

Thus the argument from the Covenant necessarily implies the
principle of biblical typology and progressive revelation. Everything in the Old Testament can be seen as expressing or conducing
to that faith in Christ which has always been the only way of
salvation.

This argument identifies the Church with the historic line of the

----

[7] 15, 429–30: II, x, 2.
[8] 15, 451: II, xi, 2.

chosen people in the Old Testament. 'The same church existed among them', as Calvin says. The Covenant with Abraham is seen as 'the solemn covenant of the church', and Calvin especially emphasizes the promise of continuity which that Covenant contains: 'I shall be your God, and the God of your descendants after you' (Gen. 17:7).[9] 'As *Calvin* hath well observed,' writes the Presbyterian John Geree, 'by virtue of this promise the Church was settled in *Abraham's* family, and it was separated from the rest of the world, as light from darkness: And the people of *Israel* (*Abraham's* posterity) was the house and sheepfold of God; And other Nations like wild beasts, ranging without in the Wilderness of the World.'[10] The Church as deriving from the Covenant with Abraham is a 'house' in the sense, often found in the Old Testament, of a line of descent from generation to generation. In this respect the 'house and sheepfold of God' is not so much the product of edification by the Spirit as it is the historic vehicle of the Spirit. John Cotton points out that 'the promise was not only to the repenting and believing Israelites, nor only to their children repenting and believing; but God had promised also to pour his Spirit upon their children that they might repent and believe.' 'It is to the same purpose', he adds, 'that upon the repentance and faith of *Zachaeus*, the Lord pronounceth salvation to be unto his house, *Luke* 19.9. This day (saith he) salvation is come to this house, forasmuch as he also is the son of *Abraham*: which is not only in respect of the Religious care, which *Zachaeus* would take to teach his household the way of salvation, but also in respect of the Covenant, by which not only *Zachaeus* was bound to teach his household, but the Lord also had bound himself to bless the means of salvation to his household.'[11] The argument from the Covenant comes to replace the theory of apostolic succession as the basis of historic continuity in the Church. It provides biblical assurance that God has 'bound himself to bless the means of salvation' carried down through the ages by a historic institution.

The Church is a large family, and, conversely, as the Separatist Henry Ainsworth observes, 'families . . . being well ordered, and conjoined in the faith of Christ, are as little Churches, so called by [Rom. 16:5; 1 Cor. 16:19] the Apostle; and ought to have care,

---

[9] 15, 387: II, viii, 21.
[10] 47, 10.
[11] 25, 48.

whatsoever be done in others, that [Josh. 24:15; Gen. 35:2] God's true worship be continued in them.'[12] The doctrine of the Covenant, Cotton says,

> may teach every righteous Householder and Parent, to take more care to leave a good covenant to their children and servants than anything else. If they have but this portion left to them, they shall do well, whether they grow and prosper in the things of this world or no. God hath made a *Covenant* with the Parents and Householders, and it shall descend upon them so far as God doth order it.[13]

Just as Abraham was commanded to circumcise his whole family as 'a token of the Covenant', so the Christian sacraments are seals of membership in the Christian family. John Ball, a Presbyterian, explains: 'The Sacraments are the seals of the Covenant to the faithful, which is the form of the Church, and when for substance rightly used, tokens and pledges of our spiritual admittance and entertainment into the Lord's family, and Symbols or testimonies whereby the people of God are distinguished from all other Nations.'[14] The two kinds of Christian family are not merely analogous; the Covenant, 'which is the form of the Church', passes down through both by the same hereditary right, so that the Church becomes an extension of the civil family relationship. Separatists like Ainsworth, Congregationalists like Cotton, Presbyterians, and indeed Anglican Conformists all argue from the Covenant with Abraham that members by birth, adoption, or servant status in a particular Christian family belong *ipso facto* to the Church. Only anti-paedobaptists like John Saltmarsh object that 'Baptism is not to be received by *Generation* now, as *Circumcision* was, but by *Regeneration* or *visible* Profession, as at first: Nor are the *carnal seed* now any more *children* of *Abraham*, but the *Faithful*.'[15]

This antithesis of generation and regeneration aptly expresses the basic antinomy of Paul's thought concerning the Church. Saltmarsh and others who associate baptism exclusively with regeneration faithfully reproduce the emphasis of Paul's thought concerning the rite itself, but they do so by renouncing an aspect

---

[12] I, 393.
[13] 23, 26.
[14] 4, 19.
[15] 100, 8.

of its significance for the Church which Paul himself does not renounce.

Baptism figures from before the time of Paul's apostleship as the normal rite of entry into the community of believers in the risen Christ. The original community appears to have associated its baptism with that performed by John the Baptist; but where John's baptism could only signify repentance in view of the eschatological 'wrath to come' upon the world, Christian baptism was 'with the holy spirit' (Mark) or 'in the holy spirit and in fire' (Matthew, Luke), initiating believers into present participation in the fulfilment of eschatological hope. John's message included a warning, 'And think not to say within yourselves, We have Abraham to our father: for I say unto you, that God is able of these stones to raise up children unto Abraham' (Matt. 3:9), but that kind of warning was by no means new to the traditions of Israel, and it was certainly not intended or understood to invalidate the historical transmission of God's promise to his people. On the contrary, John may well have been adopting the institution of proselyte baptism to his prophetic purpose: to call on Jews to undergo the same purification rite that others performed in order to become Jews might be a very compelling prophetic dramatization of the warning that they had fallen off from the Covenant and must now return to it.[16] Far from abrogating the kind of communal identity which is based upon the filiation of God's promise to his people from generation to generation, John's conception of baptism remains entirely within the tradition which maintains that identity. There is no reason to doubt that the original Christian community also conceived of itself in this way.

That it did do so would seem to be the natural inference from the words of Peter to those who had been moved by his sermon on the day of Pentecost, a text which figures prominently in the arguments for infant baptism:

Now when they heard this, they were pricked in their heart, and said unto Peter and to the rest of the apostles, Men and brethren, what shall we do? Then Peter said unto them, Repent, and be baptized every one of you in the name of Jesus Christ for the remission of sins, and ye shall receive the gift of the Holy Ghost. For the promise is unto you, and to

[16] See W. F. Flemington, *The New Testament Doctrine of Baptism* (41, 15–17). The present discussion is indebted principally to Flemington's study and to Rudolf Schackenburg, *Baptism in the Thought of St. Paul* (102).

your children, and to all that are afar off, even as many as the Lord our God shall call (Acts 2:37-9).

A Hebrew speaking to Hebrews, Peter might well be expected to add 'and to your children' when he spoke of God's promise; he need not be supposed to have given thought to any complications which so natural and obvious a phrase might eventually lead to. The real question is not whether this text shows that Peter actually baptized children—orthodox defenders of paedobaptism do not claim that it does—but whether there is any meaning at all in Peter's words, 'and to your children'. As Stephen Marshall points out, 'except in relation to the Covenant, there was no occasion to name their *children*; it had been sufficient to have said, a promise is made to *as many as the Lord shall call*.'[17] 'For even the children of pagans (whilst their children remain Pagans) have the promise belonging to them, as soon as themselves do repent and believe,' Cotton observes; 'And what more have the children of believers belonging to them than so?'[18] Peter and his hearers would have understood the question.

Paul never speaks of baptism expressly 'in relation to the Covenant', but his argument from the Covenant with Abraham shows that the principle of communal identity which Peter's words to his new converts express remains essential to Paul's thought. While he sees in baptism the significance of participation in Christ's death and resurrection and develops a conception of the Church as living and growing by the work of the Spirit which follows upon regeneration, he by no means abandons the earlier Church's conception of itself as renewing the line of descent from Abraham. The enduring identity thus defined is not merely the perpetual recurrence of a certain phenomenon, like the recurrence of the cycle of growth and decay in nature, but a unique historical continuity.

---

[17] 67, 17. The present discussion assumes, as did seventeenth-century theologians, of course, that the words ascribed to Peter in this passage in Acts represent a basically reliable record. This assumption is supported by Flemington, pp. 43-5, with particular respect to the mention of baptism. However, for present purposes it makes little difference whether the mention of baptism is authentic or was added later, for the essential conflict between two conceptions of the nature of the community is implicit in the Pentecostal situation itself. If the imminent expectation of the Parousia kept that conflict from concerning the original community, there might be a certain 'rightness' in the fact, supposing it is so, that the words about baptism which have the effect of calling attention to that conflict were added later.

[18] 25, 28.

This side of Paul's total conception of the Church is abandoned if Church membership no longer passes down from generation to generation, as it did in the time of the Old Testament, but springs up in every age without genealogy, so to speak, 'by *Regeneration* or *visible* Profession, as at first'.

To maintain these two conceptions of the Church together requires either that infants should be 'taken into Covenant with their parents in respect of saving Graces', which, as John Geree says, 'is so manifestly against Protestants' principles and experience, that no Protestant can hold it', or else that the Church should include many unregenerate persons. 'So we conceive', Geree concludes,

> that now under the Gospel by virtue of the same Covenant, (into participation of which believing Christians are assumed, as children of *Abraham*), they with their seed make up the visible Kingdom of Christ, and enjoy outward privileges. And the elect amongst them enjoy those things in truth, which others only have externally and in profession. And this is to be presumed of all the Infants of believers, till they discover the contrary.[19]

The distinction between the visible Church and the invisible is seen to extend back through the Old Testament to the time of Abraham. 'And this will yet more fully appear', as Stephen Marshall puts it,

> if we consider how St. *Paul* to the *Galatians* shows that the *same seed* of *Abraham*, so much spoken of in the Covenant made with him, is now found among the Gentiles, as it was formerly among the Jews; there you shall find *three sorts* of *Abraham's* seed: First, *Christ*, *Gal.* 3.16, the root and stock, the head, and elder brother of all the rest. Secondly, all *true believers* are *Abraham's* seed, 3.29; these only are made partakers of the *spiritual* part of the Covenant. Thirdly, you shall find another seed of *Abraham*, who were only circumcised in the *flesh*, and not in the *heart*, who though they were either *born* of *Abraham's* seed, or *professed* *Abraham's* faith, and so were Jews *facti*, though not *nati*, *made*, though not *born Jews*, becoming Proselytes, never came to make *Abraham's* God their All-sufficient portion, but placed their happiness in somewhat which was not *Christ*, either by *seeking justification by the works of the Law, being ignorant of God's righteousness, and going about to establish their own righteousness did not submit themselves unto the righteousness of God* [Rom. 10:3], or placed their happiness, *in satisfying the lusts of the*

flesh, going a whoring after the Creature; and so though they were *Abraham's* seed by *profession* and *outward cleaving* to the Covenant, yet were to be cast off with the rest of the uncircumcised, of whom *Ishmael* and *Esau* were types, Gal. 4.22. etc. *Even so it is now in the* times of the Gospel. . . .[20]

Ishmael and Esau are the standard examples to show that those who are 'called, but not chosen' are indeed 'in the Church for a while,' as Ainsworth explains, 'but not of it'.[21] The narrative of the lives of Ishmael and Esau makes their predestined reprobation clear from the beginning, but both were circumcised according to the Covenant as being of the family of Abraham. Not their predestined reprobation, then, or even any sins they committed—for whatever these were they were certainly no greater than those attributed to a Jacob or a David, or indeed to Abraham himself— but the fact that they 'did discovenant themselves'[22] accounts for their being cast out of the Church along with their descendants. As Cotton explains, 'the one mocked at the Heir of the Covenant, and the other despised the Birth-right of the Covenant; and so the one was cast out, and the other withdrew himself from the fellowship of the Church, and both of them deprived their children of *Circumcision*.'[23] But that an Ishmael or an Esau was cast out, observes the Presbyterian Thomas Blake, 'sufficiently argues he was once in'.[24]

Ishmael and Esau are unusual, however, in that their cases are clear. They are not hypocrites. Most of the Church's unregenerate membership will always consist of those whom Stephen Marshall describes as 'a holy seed by *external profession, Gal.* 4.29. who either with the false Teachers which *Paul* there speaks of, mingle *justification by the Law and Gospel together*, or with others, 2 *Tim.* 3.5. though they have *a form of godliness, yet deny the power of it in their lives and conversations*'.[25] These do not 'discovenant themselves', but rather, as Cotton says, 'they are like the Seed of the *Israelites*, who though many of them were not sincerely godly, yet whilst they held forth the public Profession of God's People (*Deut.* 26.3 to 11.) and continued under the wing of the Covenant and subjection to the Ordinances, they were still accounted an *holy*

[20] 67, 13–14.
[21] 1, Sig. Hh8–Hh8ᵛ.
[22] 25, 44.
[23] 22, 12.
[24] 8, 247.
[25] 67, 14.

Seed (Ezr. 9.2.) and so their children were Partakers of *Circum-cision.*[26] Far from representing a regrettable compromise with the conditions of life in this world, the presence of such people in the Church is essential to its nature as based on the Pauline argument from the Covenant. To attempt to exclude them would not be merely impractical; it would be a denial of the identity of the Church with the chosen people of the Old Testament. No one believing in infant baptism—certainly neither Calvin nor anyone representative of English Separatism, Congregationalism, or Pres-byterianism—ever entertained the notion which Perry Miller ascribes to all of these people, that the ideal polity 'would be to gather churches exclusively of the elect, so that the roll-call of the Church Militant might be made identical with that of the Church Triumphant . . .'.[27] That would be to quarrel with the historic dispensation of grace.

Explaining 'how the carnal seed of *Abraham* might then, and may now partake (after a sort) in the Covenant of grace, and in the seal of the Covenant of grace, and yet fall away from grace: and nevertheless their falling from grace be no countenance to the *Arminian* error of apostasy from grace', Cotton writes:

There is a double state of grace, one adherent, (which some not unfitly call federal grace) sanctifying to the purifying of the flesh, *Heb.* 9.13. another inherent, sanctifying of the inner man. And of this latter there be two sorts: one, wherein persons in Covenant are sanctified by com-mon graces, which make them serviceable and useful in their callings, as *Saul, Jehu, Judas,* and *Demas,* and such like hypocrites. Another whereby persons in Covenant are sanctified unto union and communion with Christ and his members in a way of regeneration and salvation. In respect of adherent or federal grace, all the children of a believing parent are holy, and so in an estate of grace. In respect of inherent common graces, *Saul, Jehu,* and *Judas* and *Demas* were sanctified of God to their several callings for the service of his people, as Apostates may be, *Heb.* 10.29. Now there is no doubt but men may fall away from adherent federal grace, as also from inherent common graces; and yet without any prejudice to the perseverance of sincere believers, and without any countenance to the *Arminian* error or Apostasy from grace, to wit, from such grace as accompanieth salvation. And as for the cir-cumcision of *Ishmael* (and such as he) it was a sign and seal of the righteousness of faith, not of that which he had received, but of that

---

[26] 22, 12.
[27] 73, 54.

which God offered to apply to him in the use of the means of grace in *Abraham's* family . . .[28]

That God bestows 'common' graces for various purposes to many people who are not to receive 'such grace as accompanieth salvation' is a conspicuous point in Calvin's teaching,[29] but this theory of 'federal' grace is a variation on the idea which does not appear in Calvin. It is evidently intended to clarify a question which Calvin never clearly addresses himself to: what, precisely, is holy about those persons who are 'accounted an holy seed' although predestined to reprobation? In order to guard against the natural inclination of such persons to find comfort in the performance of 'things sanctified by the law of the Lord', Calvin warns that 'by handling something sacred, the unclean hand profanes it'.[30] Cotton undoubtedly agrees with this dictum with respect to the ultimate interest of the persons themselves, but his emphasis in discussing 'federal grace' is on the 'holy seed' collectively. In order to explain its holiness even in its unregenerate members, he has recourse to the theory of 'common' graces, simply specifying that God dispenses these especially to his Church. Thus where Calvin cites Saul along with such pagan exemplars as Camillus to illustrate the operation of common graces in the unregenerate,[31] Cotton lists Saul along with other biblical figures 'sanctified of God to their several callings for the service of his people' but themselves not ultimately saved. Such people are like priests, whose service is holy whatever the state of their souls. Unregenerate members of the Church have

only gifts of Tongues, and utterance, and a common Faith; which things are not that Sanctification which is a fruit of saving Faith, but only such gifts as do sanctify them unto the work of the Ministry perhaps, or Magistracy, and fit them for household Government, or the

---

[28] 25, 43.

[29] See *Institutes*, II, ii, 17, and McNeill's notes on that place (15, 276).

[30] 15, 775: III, xiv, 7.

[31] 15, 293–4: II, iii, 4. How slight an extension of Calvin's dicta concerning 'common' and 'special' graces is necessary to produce the category of 'federal' grace appears in a remark in the *Institutes* concerning Judas. At one point Christ 'numbers Judas among the elect, although he "is a devil" [John 6:70]. This refers only to the office of apostle, which, even though it is a clear mirror of God's favor, as Paul often acknowledges in his own person [e.g., Gal. 1:16; Eph. 3:7], still does not contain in itself the hope of eternal salvation' (15, 941: III, xxii, 7).

like; and so much Positive work there is in them as doth make them in some measure fit for the work or service they are called to.[32]

Cotton does not hesitate to conclude from the Covenant with Abraham that God sanctifies hypocrisy in the seed of Abraham.

This appreciation of 'common' graces would seem to be a distinctive feature of Cotton's theology. 'I have heard (I confess) you stand much upon common graces', his critic, William Twisse, tells him,

But what they are, and to what end they tend, and whether absolutely or conditionally imparted according to your opinion: when I shall be sufficiently informed, I will do my best endeavor to weigh them in the balance of Christian and Scholastical examination, and accordingly to give them that due respect which belongs to them.[33]

Twisse's suspicion is aroused especially by Cotton's description of 'the grace of redemption' as

offering the death of Christ, and reaching forth some fruits thereof unto all, as the promising and offering sufficient help to bring them to the knowledge of God and means of grace: yea, and sometime bestowing on them the participation of some excellent and common graces. . . .[34]

To say that people who have not accepted the offered death of Christ may nevertheless receive 'some excellent and common graces' as 'fruits thereof' seems nonsense to Twisse. What he neglects, however, is Cotton's interest in accounting for the state of those people who practice 'obedience to Christ and walking worthy of him' to the best of their ability as something 'commanded in the Law'.[35] That it is so commanded can hardly be denied, 'For if the infidelity and disobedience of the men of this

---

[32] 26, 44.
[33] 113, 265.
[34] 113, 259–60.
[35] 113, 260. Cf. *Institutes*, III, ii, 11 (15, 555): 'I know that to attribute faith to the reprobate seems hard to some, when Paul declares it the result of election [cf. 1 Thess. 1:4–5]. Yet this difficulty is easily solved. For though only those predestined to salvation receive the light of faith and truly feel the power of the gospel, yet experience shows that the reprobate are sometimes affected by almost the same feeling as the elect, so that even in their own judgment they do not in any way differ from the elect [cf. Acts 13:48]. Therefore it is not at all absurd that the apostle should attribute to them a taste of the heavenly gifts [Heb. 6:4–6]—and Christ, faith for a time [Luke 8:13]; not because they firmly grasp the force of spiritual grace and the sure light of faith, but because the Lord, to render them more convicted and inexcusable, steals into their minds to the extent that his goodness may be tasted without the Spirit of adoption.'

world to the Gospel of Christ be sin . . . then the contrary virtues are commanded in the Law' (113, 260). Moreover, the effort to obey Christ undoubtedly produces in some unregenerate people's lives a closer approach than they would otherwise have made to the perfection of the Law, which argues that God 'offereth them in Christ greater grace and helps to keep [the Law] than after the fall they could have attained unto without Christ'. Of course, even with these helps, the closest approach which fallen human beings can make to perfection still comes pitifully short, and virtuous Christians are therefore as surely damned under the Law as virtuous pagans unless at some point they receive 'the grace of redemption' itself. In the meantime, none the less, they have been sanctified in a way that distinguishes them from virtuous pagans. By their participation in the Church they have received 'sufficient help to bring them to the knowledge of God and means of grace'— which, to be sure, only means that they are without excuse if they do not ultimately come to saving faith—, and by their 'excellent and common graces' they have carried on the historical mission of the chosen people.

This conception of 'federal grace' supplements the commonplace precept that by 'a certain charitable judgment', as Calvin says, 'we recognize as members of the church those who, by confession of faith, by example of life, and by partaking of the sacraments, profess the same God and Christ with us.'[36] Cotton can go somewhat further in valuing Church fellowship with people whose virtues are such as to tax charity. 'For a little more explaining of this' he ventures at one point upon a wry bit of scriptural allegory. 'Of Hypocrites,' he says, 'there are two sorts (and you shall find them in the Church of God): some are washed Swine, others are Goats':

The *Swine* are those of whom our Saviour Christ saith, *That they return unto their wallowing in the mire*; like unto these are such men who at the hearing of some Sermon have been stomach sick of their sins, and have rejected their wicked courses, but yet the swine's heart remaineth in them, as a Swine when he commeth where the puddle is, will readily lie down in it . . . But these are a grosser kind of Hypocrites.

There is another sort that go far beyond these, and they are *Goats*, so called, *Matth.* 25.32,33. and these are clean Beasts such as chew the cud, meditate upon Ordinances, and they divide the hoof, they live both

---

[36] 15, 1022–3: *Institutes*, IV, i, 8.

in a general and particular calling, and will not be idle; they are also fit for sacrifice; what then is wanting? Truly they are not *sheep* all this while, they are but *Goats*, yet a Goat doth loath that which a Swine will readily break into; but where then do they fall short of the nature of sheep? A difference there is, which standeth principally in these particulars.

As he proceeds to the particulars, it is hard not to wonder if he is describing some of the builders of the Bay Colony. In this Calvinist, it would seem, theology and temperament happily combine to produce an ironic forbearance towards the pillars of society that might almost be called Chaucerian:

The Goat is of a Capricious nature, and affecteth Eminency, his gait also is stately: *Prov.* 30.30. *Agur* reckoneth the He-goat among the 4 things that are comely in going. And they are full of Ambition, they cannot abide swamps and holes, but will be climbing upon the tops of mountains; there is not that plain lowly sheepish frame that attendeth unto the voice of the Shepherd, to be led up and down in fresh pastures: they attend upon their ends, and will outshoot God in his own Bow, and therefore when they have done many things for Christ, he will say unto them, *Depart from me, ye workers of iniquity*. More Eminency they did affect, than they were guided unto. . . . yet notwithstanding, you may receive a Goat into Church-fellowship for all his capricious nature, and he will be a clean creature, and of much good use.

The idea of 'federal grace' helps Cotton to suffer goats more or less gladly, though he adds at the end: 'They are of a Rankish nature all of them, specially the old Goats will have an unsavory relish, far from that pleasant sweetness that is in a sheep. . . .'[37]

These Typhoid Marys of grace show that the visible Church is not simply a temporal figure of the timeless invisible Church. The holiness of Church members does not reflect predestination directly but as a function of God's inexplicable purpose of using historical and social means to gather his elect. His revealed promise to do so is the Covenant upon which the Church is formed. It means that the calling of many is sanctified as instrumental to the choosing of some.

Thus Paul's argument from the Covenant with Abraham leads to a conception of the Church complementary to that which develops out of the theme of edification. The one establishes the identity of the Church in history; the other conceives of the identity of the

[37] 26, 44–7.

Church as that of a vital process in the present. The one shows a difference in kind between the new communal order of the Church and other forms of social order, and insists on its separation from them; the other attaches the Church to the most fundamental of social institutions, the family. The one sees the Church as the creation of the Spirit, the other as its vehicle.

The first 'planting' of a church may be seen as the resolution of all these antinomies. The first 'builders' of reformed churches may repeat in some sort the experience envisioned by Paul for that unique generation to whom his message is addressed. Those who hear the promise which has been carried down through the ages to the time when its meaning is revealed to them are 'grafted', as Paul says (Rom. 11:16 ff.), into the line of descent from Abraham. The Covenant by which they 'hold together' in the profession of their faith makes them partakers in the Covenant with Abraham. The 'house' of Abraham passes into the living temple as a melodic line might be concluded in a triumphant chord. The latent difficulties of adapting to a historical situation a set of conceptions describing a peculiar eschatological one may readily be passed over, as in the letter of the Frankfurt congregation; or possibly they may play some part in the formation of actual eschatological expectations. These difficulties make themselves felt, however, in the dissensions which soon develop within English Puritanism.

The problem of Puritan polity can be summarized in Saltmarsh's cogent terms as that of relating 'generation' to 'regeneration' in a concept of the Church. Saltmarsh understands Paul's announcement that the 'uncircumcision' is to inherit the promise as meaning that the line of 'generation' ended with the coming of Christ; 'Nor are the *carnal seed* now any more *children of Abraham*, but the *Faithful*.' Down to the time of Christ the promise was conveyed in a historical institution, the family of Abraham; since that time the Spirit can fend for itself historically. Covenants with the family or the nation as such, Saltmarsh says,

in their right nature were a *dispensation* more of the *Old Testament-strain*; a National Church had a Covenant to gather them up into their National *way* of *worship*, and were under the *Laws* of an *external Pedagogy*; and now the *spiritual dispensation* being come, even the *Gospel* of *Jesus Christ*, there is a fulness of *spirit* let out upon the *Saints* and *people* of *God*, which gathers them up more *closely*, *spiritually*, and *cordially*, than the *power* of any former *dispensation* could: the very

Covenant of *God* himself, of which the former were *typical* and *Prophetical*, comes in nakedly upon the *spirits* of his, and draws them in, and is a *law* upon their *inward parts*, sweetly compelling in the *consciences* with *power*, and yet not with *force*; with *compulsion*, and yet with *consent*; and surely where this *Covenant* of *God* hath its *kindly* and *spiritual* operation, there would need no such *external supplement* as before....[38]

The Church in the New Dispensation does not have or need the kind of temporal dimension it needed and had in the Old. It is disengaged from 'carnal' history. All the generations of believers since the first coming of Christ are to the lineage of Abraham as a single, 'last' generation in a strange interval of non-historical time before the end of time.

Thus the idea of the Church as a living process in the present can be affirmed by simply relegating the Church's temporal continuity to the Old Dispensation. To preserve the temporal component, on the other hand, conservative Puritans assert that generation and regeneration correspond, not to the Old Dispensation and the New, but to the visible Church and the invisible. Generation establishes the historical identity of the visible Church, regeneration the timeless identity of the invisible. However, this solution, too, proves unsatisfactory. The demand that the visible Church should be based on regeneration cannot really be set aside simply by pointing out that only the invisible Church is perfectly so. On the contrary, by formulating the idea of the invisible Church in Pauline terms as the perfection of the process of edification, Saltmarsh can make the fact that the perfection is invisible a compelling argument to show that the process itself must be visible:

The *invisible* or *mystical* Church is made up of *pure living stones*; all is *spiritual* ... and as it is here, in this *spiritual, invisible, glorious building*; so it is in the *outward, visible Communion* below, or *building* here, which is the *Image* of that above: The *Temple* here is according to that *Pattern* there; and as that is of *true, real, essentially spiritual living stones*; so the *Church* here is to consist of such as *visibly, formally,* and *outwardly* appear so....[39]

The Church cannot be visibly carried forward by generation and 'invisibly' constituted by regeneration, for that would be to sever the process from its end.

[38] 100, 71.
[39] 100, 69–70

Some, therefore, like Saltmarsh, gladly allow the history of the work of redemption to be swallowed up in endless eschatology; others quietly allow the theme of edification to lapse, as has been seen. Between these apparently exclusive alternatives, however, there appears a third 'Church way', the Congregational, which claims to combine 'generation' and 'regeneration' in the visible, present form of the Church.

This claim is implicit from the beginning in the fact that Separatist and Congregational churches are formed, strictly speaking, not by the first making of a covenant, but by the renewal of one. The open profession by which Brownist congregations 'hold together' is not sealed by baptism where the covenanting members have already received that sacrament, albeit in that very Church from which they are separating themselves because they consider it false. They do not consider themselves as new converts but as the seed of Abraham turning again to the Lord after a period of apostasy. The biblical model for their situation is not the conversion and mass baptism that followed Pentecost; nor is it the calling of Abraham into Covenant, when he circumcised his family. They look back, rather, to those repeated acts of Covenant renewal instituted by the good kings of Judah in the time of the Divided Monarchy. Browne argues, for example, that King Hezekiah rightly declined to chastise the people of Israel in his own time for their manifest violations of the Covenant, 'for they had not received the covenant, but their forefathers, and they were now called to the covenant again, which the Lord had disannulled with their forefathers: as it is written [2 Chron. 15], that for a long season Israel had been without the true God, and without Priest to teach, and without law.'[40] Until they had been 'called to the covenant again' they could not be treated as the people of the Covenant. In like manner, a company of baptized Christians, when they have been 'for a long season . . . without the true God, and without Priest to teach, and without Law', must renew the Covenant whereby they form a church. 'Solemn and explicit renewal of the Covenant is a Scripture Expedient for Reformation' declares the synod held in New England nearly a century later (1679), when a later generation of Congregationalists seems to be slackening its hold on the Covenant; and still it is the good kings of Judah who show the way:

[40] 13, 162.

When the Church was overrun with Idolatry and Superstition, those whom the Lord raised up as Reformers, put them upon solemn Renewal of Covenant. So Asa, Jehojadah, Hezekiah, Josiah. By a parity of Reason, when Churches are overgrown with worldiness (which is spiritual Idolatry) and other corruptions, the same course may and should be observed in order to Reformation.[41]

The New Englanders consider their present crisis to be extraordinary in degree, but not in kind; their prescription is simply for an especially solemn and explicit performance of that open profession which constitutes 'Edification and Reformation' at all times:

It seems to be most conducive unto Edification and Reformation, that in Renewing Covenant, such things as are clear and indisputable be expressed, that so all the Churches may agree in Covenanting to promote the Interest of holiness, and close walking with God.[42]

This later-day crisis in New England brings out clearly a paradox in Congregational theology of the Church which is already present by implication in Browne's acceptance of infant baptism: the life of the Church consists of the renewal at every moment of a covenant that was never broken.

In effect, then, the problem of reconciling 'generation' with 'regeneration' as the principle of the Church's identity is recast in Old Testament terms. To become 'overgrown with worldiness' is to sink back into that bondage to the 'dead and beggarly elements' which marks the failure of life in the Church; it can also be seen as a failure to maintain the Covenant relationship which constitutes the chosen people. This manner of equating the pressures of worldly life with the circumambient powers which threatened the very existence of Israel is not, after all, merely an allegorical imposition on the Old Testament, which recognizes clearly enough the danger for Israel of acculturation in its commerce with the nations of the world. For the whole people it is the danger of

---

[41] 117, 435. Of course, it is only 'by a parity of Reason' or by analogy that the situation of the New England congregations is said to be like that of the false church from which their forefathers departed. Their falling off consists of 'corruption in manners (though not in Worship)', and the new reformers go on to imply a distinction between 'Renewal' and 'Renovation of Covenant' (p. 436). However, the distinction is not insisted on; and in view of the close relation in Congregationalist thought between worship and 'close walking with God', it would not seem to be an essential difference.

[42] 117, 437.

death; the admonition to obey the statutes of a jealous God 'that ye may live' applies in the first instance to the collective existence of the people as a people. This is the great lesson invariably illustrated by the Deuteronomic chronicle of the Divided Monarchy, in which Congregationalists find their models of reformation and Covenant renewal; yet even in that chronicle, and in Deuteronomy itself, but most powerfully in Hosea and Jeremiah, that lesson is combined with the assurance of God's enduring interest in his chosen people. The life of the people hangs on their ever-renewed loyalty to the God of the Covenant, and yet their continuing identity as the chosen people rests upon something far more reliable than their own performance. This double awareness of the Covenant relationship with God, compounded of perpetual assurance and precarious immediacy, underlies the recurrent ritual of Covenant renewal in the Old Testament, as it does the polity of seventeenth-century Congregationalism.

That polity is the most complete expression of Puritan ecclesiology. It does not resolve the conflicts in which the Puritan tradition acts out, as it were, the basic antinomies of Pauline thought concerning the Church; it does better—it maintains them, and in doing so maintains for a season the vitality of that uniquely Christian communal experience which the early Puritans found described in the words of Paul. Finally, when the problems of Church polity are elaborated in terms of the receiving and renewing of covenants, they are drawn into the fundamental dialectic in which Puritans come to see the most comprehensive unifying principle of the Bible. Church polity becomes an aspect of Covenant, or Federal, Theology.

V

THE COVENANT OF GRACE

CALLED to preach before the newly crowned King Charles I, Richard Senhouse chose as his text 'Revel. 2. vers. 10. the last words. *And I will give thee a Crown of life.*' He begins with an encomium of 'and':

And. As St. Bartholomew is by *Dionysius* quoted to have said of Divinity, καὶ πόλλην καὶ ἐλαχίστην, & *magnam esse* & *minimam,* that it was both great & little; so this same *And* here, though little in the sentence, yet great in sense: me thinks, like that πηδάλιον in St. *James,* the Helm, which though it be small, yet turneth about the whole ship: as a drop, a pearl indeed, and yet a chain of pearl too, connecting here together man's duty, *Be faithful,* and God's bounty, *I will give thee.* As if on these two, *officium* & *beneficium,* hung all the Law and the Prophets, as *Gregory* spake elegantly of Christ, γεφυρώσας, that he joined heaven and earth together as with a bridge; this *And* here being a conjunction of both, standing here like *Jacob's* ladder upon the earth, *Be ye faithful;* and the top of it reaching up to heaven, *The Crown of life.* Or as he wittily called the circle of the Moon *Isthmus,* an Island twixt eternity and generation: this little *And* here, like a little Island, on the one hand bordering upon the Church militant, on the other upon the Church triumphant, conjoining here to man's Christian practice of being faithful, Christ's gracious *And* of promise. . . .[1]

Yet some there are who reject this little syntactical Christ figure: 'That which here is propounded conditionally, they presume upon absolutely, and so make reckoning to go up to heaven in some whirlwind; or as passengers at sea, to be brought to heaven even sleeping: to win heaven without working, to be crowned without striving, laying claim to this obligation, without ever looking to its condition.'[2] Whatever Charles' convictions concerning his earthly crown, he evidently approved the 'Protestant ethic' with respect to the heavenly one: 'Do well and have well, do this and live,

---

[1] 107, 743–4.
[2] 107, 744.

believe and be saved, be religious and reign, be faithful and be crowned: *And I will give thee a Crown of life.* A gracious covenant sure. . . .'[3]

Less elegantly but with equal conviction, Robert Browne also proclaims the gospel of 'and': 'As again it is written, *Walk before me, and be thou upright, and I will make my covenant between me and thee* [Gen. 17:1–2]. As who [should] say, one condition and part of the covenant is our upright and good profession.'[4] The courtly preacher is berating Antinomians, and the reformer without tarrying for any is condemning the Church in which Senhouse is ordained, explaining that 'the word is not the covenant to establish a Church except it reign and rule in the Church, to subdue it in obedience to the Lord: for the Lord maketh no covenant but with those that turn from iniquity in Jacob' [Isa. 59:20]. Each takes his stand on that little bridge Senhouse speaks of, the 'and' connecting a promise with a condition to form God's 'gracious covenant'.

It is a mysterious connective, however, and in a sense which is not touched on in Senhouse's metaphysical conceits. The real mystery of it appears, rather, in the place which Browne cites, the all-important Covenant with Abraham. That 'and' which Browne makes a point of glossing there is, strictly speaking, not quite there at all. In Genesis 15 (the account of the 'J' version) God does not so much as mention any obligations on Abraham's part: 'That day Yahweh concluded a covenant with Abram, saying, "To your offspring I give this land . . .".'[5] In the 'P' version (Gen. 17), God first approaches Abram, saying: 'I am El Shaddai. Follow my ways and be blameless.' Then the Covenant is announced: 'I will grant a covenant between myself and you, and will make you exceedingly numerous.' Since the command precedes the Covenant, a mind formed by later-day legal traditions may assume a connection of '*officium & beneficium*' between the two utterances—'As who [should] say, one condition and part of the covenant is our upright and good profession'—but strictly speaking there is no connection. Then, in setting forth the Covenant itself, God assigns a duty to Abraham, but still without quite making the Covenant conditional upon Abraham's performance of the duty:

God further said to Abraham, 'For your part, you must keep my covenant, you and your offspring to follow, through the ages. And this shall

---

[3] 107, 745.   [4] 13, 439.   [5] 110, 111.

be the covenant between myself and you, and your offspring to follow, which you must keep: every male among you shall be circumcised' (110,122).

Finally, God does say, 'An uncircumcised male, one who has not been circumcised in the flesh of his foreskin—such a person shall be cut off from his kin: he has broken my covenant!' (110, 123.) This still leaves the Covenant with the family of Abraham unconditional, though it establishes a condition for individual membership in the family; and even so, as those who defend infant baptism on the model of infant circumcision like to point out, the case of Ishmael proves that performance of the condition of circumcision does not obligate God with respect to the individual circumcised. Thus even the ritualistically inclined 'P' version does not quite bring the Covenant to a *quid pro quo*. The Covenant with Abraham is set forth in a way that seems to suggest the later-day meaning attached to the idea of a covenant in many other places in the Old Testament, but it ultimately resists that interpretation, as Paul points out.

Paul's argument from the Covenant with Abraham hinges on the relationship between that and the Sinai Covenant. The first, Paul insists, does not stipulate conditions; the second he identifies altogether with the conditions it contains, usually calling it simply 'the Law'. The Law, he argues, cannot condition the Covenant with Abraham since it was communicated, by his reckoning, 420 years later. That is to say that the Covenant which constitutes the chosen people of God is not conditional upon their performance. The conditions of the Sinai Covenant were communicated, paradoxically, in order to bring the people to a recognition that their Covenant with God was unconditional; for until they recognized their radical inability to fulfill God's conditions of righteousness they might imagine that they were chosen for doing so. Thus the Sinai Covenant is subordinated to the Covenant with Abraham.

The main outline of this argument cannot be overlooked by any Christian exegete, whatever he may make of the various problems it gives rise to, and Luther and Calvin can hardly be said to have neglected it. They do not notice, however, or else do not care to exploit, the possibility of elucidating Paul's argument by a simple adjustment of terminology. Paul's denial that salvation comes by 'the works of the Law' can be restated as a denial that it comes by the 'Covenant of Works' expressed in the conditions of the Sinai

Covenant. In contradistinction, the Covenant with Abraham can be termed the 'Covenant of Grace'. Thus Paul's argument from the Covenant with Abraham can be clearly stated in terms of contrasting Covenants. It is this mere rephrasing of the argument which constitutes the point of departure of a distinctive Covenant or Federal Theology.[6]

This adjustment of terminology leads directly to what appears to be an important exegetical discovery. Not only the history of Israel but the universal history of mankind since the Creation is covered by these two great Covenants of God with men. Since Paul holds the law which the Gentiles find in nature to be practically equivalent to the Law conveyed in the Sinai Covenant, the Covenant of Works can also be called the 'Covenant of Nature' and the Gentiles can be seen to be included in it. Furthermore—a crucial step—the Covenant of Works or of Nature can be carried back historically beyond Sinai to Eden. The essence of that covenant is the promise of life on condition of obedience, which is expressed simply, though negatively, in God's warning to Adam, 'But of the tree of the knowledge of good and evil, thou shalt not eat of it: for in the day that thou eatest thereof thou shalt surely die' (Gen. 2:17). Calvin calls this simply a command and a test (15, 245: II, i, 4). There is a promise of life attached to the command, however, as he goes on to say; and if he does not observe that such an arrangement amounts to a covenant between God and man, the reason may be simply that the Bible does not call it a covenant. To do so would not appear to be in itself a substantial departure either from the Bible or from Calvin.

Obedience was fully possible to Adam in his original state of integrity, and the acts and attitudes which constitute obedience did not need to be spelled out to him while his intelligence remained uncorrupted. After the Fall, life is still promised to man for obedience, and death is still the penalty for disobedience, and so the Covenant of Works remains in force. Its function, however, has changed with the change in man, as Peter Bulkeley explains:

Though now in the estate of corruption, no man attains life by the covenant of works, yet this so comes to pass, *not because the covenant is changed, but* because *we are changed*, and cannot fulfill the condition, to which the promise is made; the covenant stands fast, but we have not

[6] For the history of these developments see Gottlob Schrenk, *Gottesreich und Bund* . . . (104, 36–82).

stood fast in the covenant, but it is now become impossible to us, that we are unable to fulfill it, as the Apostle speaks, Rom. 8.3. Yea, it is the unchangeableness and stability of this covenant, which condemns all the world of sinful and ungodly men. The Law hath said, Cursed is everyone which continueth not in all things, etc. And the soul that sinneth (and flies not to the covenant of grace) shall die. This word takes hold upon them and condemns them.[7]

The simple command to Adam is thus equivalent to the whole of the Old Law, performing the function since the Fall of man which Paul ascribes to the Law, and related to the Covenant of Grace as the Law is to the Gospel. Because the covenant with Adam was 'almost obliterated and blotted out of man's heart' after the Fall, it was communicated again and spelled out at length in scripture, especially in the Law delivered to Moses at Mount Sinai.[8]

Nevertheless, the Gentiles have enough understanding of the Covenant of Nature to leave them, as Paul says, 'without excuse'. All men are by nature under the Covenant of Works, but none can fulfill its conditions. Thus the Covenant of Works gives to all men an apparent hope of life and a true fear of death which may serve to maintain some degree of order or 'legal holiness' among the reprobate, and that is all to the good as far as it goes; but the more sincerely men strive to fulfill the conditions of the Covenant of Works the more acute must be their sense of helplessness. To produce this terrible frustration is the principal purpose of the Covenant of Works with respect to the elect, for that will cause them to fly to the other Covenant, to hear and receive the free promise as Abraham did. Thus John Cotton can paraphrase the familiar Calvinist or Lutheran or simply Pauline account of conversion: 'God doth not call any into fellowship with himself in a Covenant of Grace, but ordinarily he first bringeth them into a Covenant of Works, and casteth them out of doors by a spirit of bondage and of burning, and then bringeth them in by the true door, and Jesus Christ is that door, *Joh.* 10.9.'[9] When the elect have been received into the Covenant of Grace they desire more than ever to obey the Law of God, and they receive grace to help them do so. Although their obedience is still imperfect so long as they are in this mortal life, they do not fear death because they are

[7] 14, Sig. (13)ᵛ.
[8] 14, Sig. K2ᵛ. See Excursus, below, p. 138.
[9] 26, 49–50.

in the Covenant of Grace, which is not made on condition of obedience. They obey God freely, not as fulfilling their part of a bargain: 'they are free from the Covenant of the Law,' as Cotton says, 'but not from the Commandment of it.'[10]

To set forth Paul's basic conceptions in this manner is at the same time to recognize, albeit not in the manner of modern critical scholarship, an important historic pattern in the Bible. Paul understands the content of revelation in a characteristically Hebrew manner as a function of the history of revelation, and he addresses himself to questions deeply rooted in the history of Israel. Thus the reapprehension of his thought in the Reformation leads in turn to a reapprehension of the historical experience of Israel; for in setting the Covenant with Abraham off against the Sinai Covenant Paul is focusing upon the basic internal tension which characterizes that historical experience from the time of Moses onward.

For all its insistence that God's favour toward his people is bound up with their obedience to him, the Old Testament never lapses into a religion of *do ut des*. This crucial but somewhat elusive characteristic of Old Testament theology is strikingly illuminated by George E. Mendenhall's demonstration of the similarity between the form of the Sinai Covenant and a device of imperial statecraft in Moses' time, the distinctive 'suzerainty treaty' form known from Hittite records unearthed in the twentieth century. One remarkable feature of such a treaty is its establishment of conditions within an unconditional relationship:

The primary purpose of the suzerainty treaty was to establish a firm relationship of mutual support between the two parties (especially military support), in which the interests of the Hittite sovereign were of primary and ultimate concern. It established a relationship between the two, but in its form it is unilateral. The stipulations of the treaty are binding only upon the vassal, and only the vassal took an oath of obedience. Though the treaties frequently contain promises of help and support to the vassal, there is no legal formality by which the Hittite king binds himself to any specific obligation. Rather, it would seem that the Hittite king by his very position as sovereign is concerned to protect his subjects from claims or attacks of other foreign states. Consequently for him to bind himself to specific obligations with regard to his vassal would be an infringement upon his sole right of self-determination and sovereignty. A most important corollary of this fact is the

[10] 26, 135.

emphasis upon the vassal's obligation to *trust* in the benevolence of the sovereign.[11]

The treaty contains on the one part no obligations and on the other no forfeitures. It goes without saying that the sovereign may use his overwhelming power to enforce his will exactly as before. The language of the treaty dwells on the sovereign's acts of benevolence in the past but does not bind him to anything for the future. Above all, the treaty obviously does not contemplate the dissolution of the basic relationship which it establishes. Failure of the vassal to obey the conditions of the treaty may lead to his destruction, no doubt, but not to his ceasing to belong to the sovereign. Yet the whole import of the treaty is to establish that relationship upon conditions, chiefly the first and great condition of exclusive loyalty. For political purposes the paradox is hardly worth noticing in view of the treaty's obvious practical function of promoting a sense of willing obligation in the vassal, but when the same formula is used to define the relation of God to his people it becomes a theological enigma.

In the subsequent history of Israel, perhaps almost from the first, another form of tension develops within the chosen people itself, not as a result of the paradox underlying the Mosaic Covenant, yet analogous to it. Those who have been gathered out of Egypt are aware of being a people by virtue of that experience. Even if they also have in common some memories of patriarchal lore, they owe their present collective identity chiefly to the direct impress of Moses' teaching and the experience of the Exodus, culminating in the Sinai event. During the period of wandering in the wilderness, however, and in the course of the conquest of Canaan, others learn of the great thing that Yahweh has done for his people, are instructed in the Covenant, and adhere to it. Even though regular ceremonies of Covenant renewal make the experience of the Exodus and Sinai in some sense theirs, it can hardly be so vivid for these people as for those who actually came out of Egypt. Nor can it be so decisive in forming their sense of collective identity as it must be for the 'mixed multitude' who have come out of bondage; for many, the story of the Exodus and the ceremonies of Covenant renewal will simply be very impressive accretions to an already substantial cultic tradition. In this difference between the

[11] 68, 30.

ways in which groups of people originally experience the Covenant may well lie the beginning of the basic internal division which runs through the subsequent history of the Covenant people.[12] One tradition emerges—or one congeries of kindred traditions—which emphasizes that the very being of the chosen people resides in their continually obeying the commandments of God's Covenant with them; another tradition emphasizes the inalienable constancy of God's promise to his people. The one tradition, that is, fastens on the conditions of the Covenant as determining the people's relation to God, while the other tends to emphasize the continuity of that relationship as deriving from God's sovereign purpose once proclaimed.

Those for whom the conditions of the Covenant are most significant especially remember Moses, who proclaimed them, while those who emphasize the sureness of the promise and its historical transmission tend to look back beyond Moses and Sinai to the Covenant with Abraham. The Mosaic tradition gives its special character to the loose, amphictyonic federation by which Israel lived in the time of the Judges. The Abrahamic tradition is apparently submerged during this early period, but its emphasis on the inheritance of the promise makes it congenial to the monarchy, so that the crucial development whereby Israel comes to have a king is marked by a reversal of the relationship between the two traditions. Mendenhall observes that

during the Monarchy and according to every indication we have in the time of David, the tradition of the covenant with Abraham became the pattern of a covenant between Yahweh and David, whereby Yahweh promised to maintain the Davidic line on the throne (II Sam. 23:5). Yahweh bound Himself, exactly as in the Abrahamic and Noachite

---

[12] Murray Lee Newman, Jr., *The People of the Covenant* (80), formulates this theory of the origin of the two covenant traditions in specific terms and traces their development in some detail. In very general terms, at least, it seems quite plausible to suppose that some such development as Newman describes did take place. To do so appears to require only two general assumptions: that the Exodus did actually take place, and is not entirely the creation of traditions dating from after the achievement of dominance in Canaan and the establishment of the amphictyony, and that the basic form of the Sinai covenant goes back, as Mendenhall appears to have demonstrated (but see Vriezen (116, 145)), to the time of the Exodus. Even if 'nihilism' should prevail with respect to these minimal assumptions concerning the historicity of the biblical narrative, the pattern of interaction between two ways of thinking about the covenant relation of God to his people would remain valuable for an understanding of the biblical account as it stands.

covenant, and therefore Israel could not escape responsibility to the king. The covenant with Abraham was the 'prophecy' and that with David the 'fulfilment.'

This was evidently accepted in the South, but not in the North. The Davidic covenant became normative in Judah—and may have been accepted eventually in the North as well, though it never succeeded in producing the stability of a single dynasty on the throne. The original center of the old Federation, understandably enough, evidently preserved far more of the old Mosaic covenant traditions.[13]

In some quarters, however, the Davidic settlement must have powerfully furthered the conviction that these conflicting traditions were inseparable. The relationship between Israel's responsibility and God's constancy reveals new depths of meaning in Hosea and Jeremiah, and a new resolve to enlist the two traditions in support of each other appears in the Josiahanic reform and Deuteronomy.

Paul's argument from the Covenant with Abraham thus resumes and claims to conclude a basic dialectic of the 'biblical process'. Paul claims that the two ways of understanding the Covenant relationship with God come together in Christ. While the conditional understanding of the Covenant is subordinated to the unconditional, Paul insists that it is not thereby invalidated: 'God forbid: yea, we establish the law' (Rom. 3:31). This assertion is the point of departure, of course, for the great debate over faith and works in the Christian tradition; so historically, at least, Paul's claim to conclusiveness has hardly been borne out. Covenant theology appears at the outset to bring a welcome new clarity to that debate by casting it in terms of the relationship between the two Covenants; what it certainly accomplishes is to trace it back into the Old Testament.

Sixteenth- and seventeenth-century theologians do not, of course, approach the Bible with the critical presuppositions or equipment to discern in it different cultural deposits, the traces of institutions and ways of thought of forgotten provenance and distinct from the normal assumptions of later-day readers. They naturally suppose that the idea of a covenant has in all times been essentially what it is in their own. It is a 'mutual agreement between parties upon Articles or Propositions on both sides, so that each party is tied and bound to perform his own conditions', as

---

[13] 68, 188–9.

Thomas Blake defines it;[14] and John Goodman points out particularly that conditions are 'as formal and essential a part of a Covenant, as any other thing belonging to it'.[15] Nevertheless, in pursuing the Pauline contrast between the two Covenants, they become very well aware of a basic strangeness in Old Testament usage. John Cotton explains:

As the heavens are higher than the earth, so are the ways of God higher than our ways, (*Isaiah.* 55.9.) and in special the ways of his grace, and of the Covenant thereof. With men indeed mutual agreement and consent is necessary to a Covenant; but with God, God's appointment maketh a Covenant, whether the creature consent to an agreement or no. God sometimes made a Covenant, and established it, not only with *Noah* and his seed, but also with the Fowls and Beasts, and every living creature, that he would never send a flood to destroy them from off the face of the earth, Gen. 9.9,10,11. And this Covenant was only an appointment of God; it did not require any consent or agreement of man, less of other creatures, to make it a Covenant. It is therefore a manifest error, to make the agreement or consent on man's part essential to a Covenant between God and man.[16]

What Cotton calls a mysterious difference between human meaning and divine is stated more concisely by William Ames as a point of sacred philology. Ames points out that

in the Scriptures every firm purpose, although it be of things without life, is called a covenant. *Jerem.* 33.20.25. My covenant of the day, and my covenant of the night: if my covenant be not with the day and night, if I appoint not the statutes of Heaven and Earth.[17]

While this perception is not presented in historical terms, it serves nevertheless to alert later-day readers to a difference between their own normal ways of thought and those implied at some important points in the Bible.

For those so instructed, the debate concerning faith and works comes to centre on the ambiguity of the Covenant idea in the Old

---

[14] 8, 3.
[15] 49, 156.
[16] 25, 64–5.
[17] 2, 101. With this biblical conception of the natural order as established upon covenants compare the *foedus naturae* in Lucretius (I, 586; II, 302; V, 57, 310, 924). In both conceptions the analogy between cosmic order and social order is explicit, but the one sees order as immanent in nature, consisting of relations 'agreed upon' by the natural or social elements themselves; in the other the only real relations are with God.

Testament. That ambiguity corresponds to the two traditions reflected in the basic scheme of Covenant Theology, but its components of conditionality and absoluteness cannot be simply identified with the Covenant of Works and the Covenant of Grace respectively. While the absoluteness of the Covenant idea is illustrated by God's covenants with the day and the night and the fowls and the beasts, that cannot be all there is to even the most unconditional expression of God's 'firm purpose' with respect to men. Thomas Gataker exclaims:

Yea, if the *Covenant of the Gospel,* that is, *of life and salvation by Christ,* be as absolute, *without any condition on man's part, as that with Noah* concerning the not drowning of the whole world again, then it is all one whether men *receive* it, and *believe* it, or no: the promise of life and salvation, and the covenant made with Christ concerning it, shall be made good unto them, as well as that made with *Noah* shall be made good unto men, whether they know it, and hear it, and believe it, or no.[18]

The central problem of Federal Theology, then, is to keep the Covenant of Grace distinct from the Covenant of Works, while still showing it to involve that sense of human response and responsibility which is expressed by the conditionality of the Covenant of Works. The full ambiguity of the biblical Covenant idea must be demonstrated in the Covenant of Grace alone.

The most obvious solution is to say simply that anyone who is in the Covenant of Grace will be moved by grace to obey God. Although this answer is undeniable in itself, and easily supportable by good Pauline texts, it does not account for the strong sense of moral exertion which Paul himself conveys. In so far as it may suggest the idea of an automatic, somnambulistic obedience to God's directions, it seems to exclude personal responsibility. Therefore the preacher bent on urging human responsibility in the Covenant without neglecting the consideration of grace may prefer to say that both Covenants are conditional, and explain the difference between them by another Pauline principle, saying that the one Covenant requires all the works of the Law, whereas in the other the only condition required of man is faith.

By comparison with the overwhelming requirements of the Covenant of Works, the simple condition of hearing and believing

[18] 45, 25.

the free offer of salvation seems, as Bulkeley observes, little enough for God to ask of man:

Some have been of mind, that the promises which we call conditional are not free promises, or promises of free grace . . .; but . . . the condition annexed (being a condition of the Gospel, not of the Law) doth no more derogate from the freeness of grace, than a Prince's offering a royal reward to a subject upon condition that he do thankfully accept of it, and acknowledge his Princely bounty towards him, doth any way derogate from the freeness of the gift; no more doth the condition of faith, by which we receive the grace given unto us of God, derogate from the freeness of his grace towards us. . . .[19]

Pursued at any length, however, this argument negates itself, as its use by John Preston strikingly illustrates. 'You will say, this is very strange,' Preston suggests:

. . . how can it be, that so small a condition as this, that to believe, should make a man partaker of the Covenant? that upon which all the promises hang initially, is nothing but believing. You see *Abraham* did no more but believe GOD, when he told him he should have a son; you see how much GOD made of that: So it is with us, if we do but believe this, God will make as much of it, he will make good all the promises of the *Covenant* to us. . . .[20]

Preston then goes on to show that the fulfilment of this one, small condition

. . . draws with it all other graces after this manner; he that believes GOD, hath a good opinion of him, he loves him; he that loves him, must needs be full of works. Besides, he that believes him, when GOD shall say to him, *I am thy exceeding great reward*, see that thou keep close to me, thou shalt have an eye upon me, and walk with me from day to day. Let a man believe that *God* is *All-sufficient*, that he will be a *Sun and a Shield* to him, and his *exceeding great reward*, he will be ready to do it. *Abraham* did so, when *God* called him from his Father's House, and from his kindred, he was ready to do so; when *God* would have him to offer up his only son, he was ready to do it: for he believed *God*, he believed his promise and his ability and willingness to help him; he believed his Almighty power, and therefore whatsoever *God* bid him do, he would do it; he preferred *God* before his own ease, before his own profit, before his only son whom he loved: Let any man believe as *Abraham* did, and of necessity it will produce good works. . . .[21]

[19] 14, Sig. Ccc (1).   [20] 91, 360–1.   [21] 91, 362.

That one 'small condition' means a life of heroic works. Preston succeeds so well in connecting faith with works that the distinction between them becomes meaningless. Not any of the remarkable gestures which manifest the imperceptible turning of the soul toward God, but that conversion itself, is the great act. The heroic works that follow from it only serve to show how difficult it is, 'small' though it may appear in ordinary human terms. It makes no real difference whether Abraham is thought of as being saved on condition of performing many great works or by that one 'small condition' of faith which implies them all.

John Saltmarsh sums up the inadequacy of this manner of distinguishing between the Covenant of Works and the Covenant of Grace:

Consider but what *straits* you bring the *Gospel* into: first, you make life appearing to be had in the *Covenant of Grace*, as at first in the *Covenant of Works*: *Do this and live*; so, *believe, repent, obey, and live*; thus runs your *Doctrine*; nor can you with all your distinctions make *Faith* in this consideration less than a *work*, and so put *Salvation* upon a *condition* of *works* again. Is this *Free-Grace*? But you say *Faith* is a gift *freely given of God*; and here is *Free-grace* still. But I pray, Is this any more *Free-Grace* respectively to what we do for life, than the Covenant of works had? All the Works wrought in us then, were freely of God, and of *free-gift* too, as Arminius well observes in the point of universal Grace; and we wrought only from a *gift given*. Either place Salvation upon a free bottom, or else you make the New Covenant but an Old *Covenant* in new terms: instead of *Do this and live, Believe this and live, repent and live, obey and live:* And all this is for want of revealing the mystery more fully.[22]

Saltmarsh's point is the same as the one that Luther made against Erasmus, that to attribute to man some small part in his own salvation is really to put salvation in his power entirely. A 'small condition' puts man in a posture of bargaining with God as surely as a 'great' one, and the Covenant of Grace comes down to nothing but a simplified Covenant of Works. As Cotton says,

. . . if thy soul be not utterly lost, so long as it hath any root, or power in itself, it is not come to an utter self-denial: though I cannot work I will believe, and if I cannot believe, I can wait that I may believe, and so here is still the old root of Adam left alive in us, whereby men seek to establish their own righteousness.[23]

[22] 101, 135.   [23] 26, 182.

To say merely that the Covenant of Grace is made on condition of faith may be only a way of training up a new sprig from the old root.

In order to guard against that consequence, Cotton declares that 'in a Covenant of works God giveth himself Conditionally; in that of grace, Absolutely.'[24] If faith is considered as a condition which man is able to fulfill for himself, it can only be a condition of the Covenant of Works. That Covenant does include a kind of faith as one of its conditions, but it is not saving faith, of which there was no need when the Covenant was made with Adam. 'The covenant of works commandeth faith in God as a creator, to preserve our being,' as Bulkeley explains, 'but not as a redeemer to deliver us from misery.'[25] Before the Fall natural religion was enough, for, as Thomas Blake says, 'Man stood then on his own bottom. His dependence was on God for being, but that being which God pleased to communicate was in that integrity and purity, that he needed not any further: But the conditions of the Covenant of Grace carry man out of himself; he must be righteous with a righteousness extrinsical, or else he will never be able to stand in judgment.'[26] The sense in which man depends on God for salvation must go beyond the sense in which he depends on God for his very being or for anything else that is found in him, including natural faith. Therefore Cotton insists: 'Faith to receive Christ is ever upon an Absolute Promise. If you will say it is a Promise to a Condition, what kind of condition was it? There is no Condition before Faith but a condition of misery, a lost condition. . . .'[27] In short, the natural human condition.

Cotton's play on the word 'condition', however, suggests a sense in which the Covenant of Grace can still be called conditional. When the word is used in connection with a covenant, it is natural to understand it as meaning something that one party to a contract agrees to perform, being fully able to do so or not, in order to bind the other party to a performance of his part. But a 'condition' can also be simply a state of being. Before conversion, as Cotton insists, man is in no condition to fulfill the condition of faith: 'there can be no gracious conditions or qualifications wrought in us before we receive union with Christ.'[28] After con-

---

[24] 26, 42.
[25] 14, Sig. K(1).
[26] 8, 72.
[27] 26, 56.
[28] 24, 2.

version man's condition is different. Then he can indeed be said to receive the promise of the Covenant of Grace upon a condition, so long as it is understood to be a 'Condition subsequent, not pre-existent, no Condition before it, whereby a man can close with Jesus Christ'.[29] Because 'our first coming on to Christ cannot be upon a Conditional but upon an Absolute Promise',[30] the Covenant of Grace must be called absolute; because our coming to Christ creates in us the condition to which the promise of salvation is made, it can also be called conditional: 'But when you read how the Lord hath made such promises to such and such qualifications, then consider that those things are indeed requisite to be found in you, but who is there in heaven or earth that can work them in you? There is none but Jesus Christ, and unless you have him to be in you, you cannot have any of these things wrought in you.'[31]

For fear of losing sight of this central point Cotton is reluctant to dwell on the conditional nature of the Covenant of Grace, but even his eager critic, William Twisse, has to admit that he is orthodox in his understanding of Covenant conditions. 'Still you proceed to prove that which no man denies,' Twisse complains: 'namely, that God purposed life to the world, upon condition of obedience and repentance'; then, unable to forego suspicion altogether, he adds: '. . . provided that you understand it aright: namely, that obedience and repentance is ordained of God as a condition of life, not of God's purpose. Otherwise it were a very wild expression to say that God ordained that obedience and repentance should be the conditions of God's purpose.'[32] Cotton evidently does understand the matter just so, and this distinction between a condition of God's purpose and a condition of life summarizes the ambiguous usage by which the Covenant terminology comes to reflect the contrasting strains in the biblical idea of man's relation to God.

Twisse, in fact, acquiesces in the Covenant terminology more readily than Cotton. Where Cotton hesitates to speak of the Covenant of Grace as a conditional promise, lest the unwary take it for a bargain like any other, Twisse insists on calling it conditional, in order to emphasize that the condition of the elect is as absolutely determined by God as any other:

And indeed, though the Purposes of God are absolute, yet his Promises are therefore conditionate, because they are conformed to the manner

---

[29] 26, 56-7.   [30] 26, 57.   [31] 26, 104-5.   [32] 113, 74-5.

of God's operation with man: For, as God works in all things agreeable
to their natures; so in man he useth to work agreeable to his nature. And
therefore, albeit his Purpose be absolute to bring them to grace and
glory, to faith and repentance, and salvation, yet he allures them to
faith and repentance by promises and threatenings. When you say that
God doth covenant and promise to give life to the Elect, out of his grace in
Christ, you might as well have said that God promiseth to give life to
them that believe and repent; and more congruously a great deal, seeing the conscience of our faith and repentance brings us to the assurance of our Election; the conscience of our Election, or of the assurance
thereof, brings us not unto faith and repentance.[33]

If someone like Saltmarsh should complain that this account leaves
faith indistinguishable from any other condition by which God
chooses to work his purposes, Twisse would not be disturbed. It
is enough for him that the absoluteness of God's purpose should
be kept ever in view. But Cotton, like Saltmarsh, insists on putting
salvation under the Covenant of Grace 'upon a free bottom', and
therefore wishes to show that the condition of saving faith manifests absolute grace in a sense in which other conditions do not.

Twisse recognizes Cotton's motive:

But it seems you desire to shape the Promises of God in the Covenant
of Grace, and in the Covenant of Works, in so different a manner, that
the one may seem to be absolute, the other conditional; whereas they
are of the same nature in both: And as God doth withal intend to give
the grace of obedience to the Elect; so doth he as absolutely intend to
deny it to the other.

Since all of God's covenants merely give effect to his absolute will,
Twisse holds that they must all be conditional in the same sense.
If obedience accompanies faith, as all must agree, then both are
conditions of the elect. To be sure, under the Covenant of Grace
God accepts imperfect obedience so long as it is sincere, which is
to say, so long as it is accompanied by faith, whereas the Covenant
of Works requires perfect obedience. But that difference does not
affect the relationship between the condition and the absolute purpose behind it; it only affects the 'conscience of our Election',
assuring us that we need not despair because our works are imperfect. Salvation itself can be said to be effected by grace only
because God's secret purpose of election is gratuitous.

[33] This and following passage: 113, 63.

Such would appear to be Twisse's version of the Federal Theology, although his self-assigned role of theological gadfly does not give occasion for a regular exposition of his own views.[34] Grace is simply a fact prior to the whole arrangement of Covenants and conditions; these merely describe the manner in which the fact is accomplished. The defence of the idea of grace is for Twisse simply a matter of keeping attention focused on the arbitrariness of God's secret will. If God's secret purpose of election is contingent upon anything, whether prior to it or subsequent but foreknown, then it is not gratuitous, not by grace. So long as election and reprobation are recognized to be absolutely arbitrary, Twisse can readily accept the Covenant scheme as a description of the revealed modalities by which they take effect. Conversely, any attempt to distinguish between them as manifesting respectively God's grace and his justice immediately incurs Twisse's suspicion. His critique of Cotton on this point is disingenuous, as will be shown, but it is illuminating as an illustration of the manner in which a preoccupation with predestination can distort Calvinism itself.

As the ultimate postulate on which the precious fact of salvation by God's free grace depends, predestination is logically the point of departure of Calvinism; psychologically, however, it does not appear as the original interest of Calvin's teaching.[35] The main thing is the message of God's special favour towards us. Cotton reflects this order of priority of motives when he lists '*Calvin's* Doctrine of Predestination, that is of grace, not faith and works

---

[34] 'Truth it is, all my writings, both printed and manuscript, that have an eye towards the press, are of a responsorious nature; but the original motive cause unto me was merely mine own satisfaction . . .' ('The Author's Epistle unto the Reader', 113, Sig. A2).

[35] John F. H. New, *Anglican and Puritan* (79, 15) goes so far as to say, 'Predestination was a minor doctrine, correlated to justification by faith alone, and to God's sovereignty.' Doubtless this is misleading with respect to the logical place of predestination in Calvinism, and it is belied by the controversies of the seventeenth century. Nevertheless, it is a just estimate of the proportional interest attached to predestination in the *Institutes*. Emile G. Léonard remarks that both 'the influence of [Calvin's] faith and the repercussions of his over-explicit theology are . . . apparent in connection with what has been wrongly regarded as his cardinal doctrine, though it certainly became so for succeeding generations—predestination' (63, 301). To the evidence which New presents to show that Elizabethan Puritans did not think of predestination as the main burden of their message may be added the testimony of Thomas Cartwright, who cites predestination as an example of true doctrine, disbelief in which does not necessarily exclude one from salvation (17, 53 ff.).

9—P.R.I.E.

foreseen' along with '*Luther's* Doctrine of Justification, that is of faith, not of works' and '*Augustine's* Doctrine of Conversion, that is of grace, and not of free-will' as forms in which the ever-new message of grace has surprised the world.[36] It was only under the pressure of theological disputation that predestination emerged as the strong point of Calvinism. The struggle against Arminianism focused attention on it especially, so that by the middle of the seventeenth century predestination had come to stand for '*Calvin's* Doctrine', even to those who, like Cotton, still understood it as a way of proclaiming the good news of grace.

When a heresy-hunter like Twisse scans the works of a preacher like Cotton for signs of compromise on predestination, he is more interested in reprobation than salvation. Cotton says that the reprobate are justly condemned under the Covenant of Works, while the elect are saved by God's free grace under the Covenant of Grace. Twisse cannot abide the distinction:

And I wonder you make not mention of the Reprobate in the latter [the Covenant of Grace], as of the Elect in the former [the Covenant of Works]: Undoubtedly, the Covenant of Works concerns all to whom it is preached; as well the Elect as the Reprobate. And the Covenant of Grace likewise concerns all to whom it is preached; as well the Reprobate as the Elect. To all it is preached, Whosoever believeth shall be saved; as well to the Reprobate as to the Elect: To all it is preached indifferently, Whosoever believeth not shall be damned; as well to the Elect as to the Reprobate: only, God shows mercy on whom he will, in giving the grace of faith; and hardens whom he will, in denying it.[37]

Cotton's argument, however, does not deny that the Covenant of Works concerns the elect or that the Covenant of Grace concerns the reprobate, but the two Covenants concern the elect and the reprobate in different ways. The Covenant of Grace is offered to both, and the elect accept it and are freed by it from the Covenant of Works, although, as has been seen, 'not from the Command of it'. The reprobate reject the Covenant of Grace and so are condemned by its condition, 'Whosoever believeth not shall be damned'; or, to put it another way, they come under the Covenant of Works, which automatically condemns them.

Cotton only claims to justify the actual condemnation of the reprobate as a fact in history. He distinguishes between this positive, historical condemnation, which does not take place 'but upon

[36] 24, 30.   [37] 113, 63–4.

sin presupposed', and the secret, original 'non-election, or preterition of the creature, according to the liberty of God's absolute
sovereignty'.[38] It is this distinction that Twisse basically objects
to. If condemnation of the creature is 'last in execution', he argues,
it must be 'first in intention'; that is, the end result of condemning
certain creatures must have been the object of God's original,
secret purpose. God must have purposed from the beginning to
condemn them, and anyone who lets slip an opportunity to say so
outright must be trying to evade the doctrine of predestination.
This suspicion is so strong in Twisse that it overrides his initially
clear perception that Cotton's argument only extends to the
modalities, the conditions, by which God's purpose is effected,
and not to the secret purpose itself. Twisse asks:

For what, I pray, is the meaning of this, God ordains none to condemnation, but upon sin presupposed? Is there any other meaning of the
words than this; God hath ordained that no man shall be condemned,
but for sin? who ever denied this? What one of our Divines, or Papists,
or of any Sect, ever called this into question? But herehence it only
follows, that sin is the cause of condemnation, and that by the ordination of God: it follows not, that sin is the cause of God's ordination;
although I confess the confusion of these is most frequent amongst our
Divines, amongst Papists, though otherwise very learned, and chiefly
among the *Arminians*, for the advantage of their cause. . . .[39]

Apparently on the assumption that the obvious meaning cannot be
what Cotton intends, for the very reason that it is obvious, Twisse
concludes, 'But I doubt not but your meaning is, in that Proposition, That sin is not only the cause of damnation, but of God's
decree also of ordaining thereunto.' From this undoubted meaning
he easily deduces Arminianism:

And if God's purpose of condemnation presuppose sin, it follows that
God's purpose of remunerating with eternal life must also presuppose
obedience; even obedience of faith, repentance, and good works; for all
these God doth remunerate with eternal life. Here appeareth the foul
tail of *Arminianism*, in the doctrine of Election, which this plausible
doctrine of yours . . . in the point of Reprobation draws after it.[40]

---

[38] 113, 42.

[39] 113, 45.

[40] 113, 46. Twisse's reaction to Cotton's concern to show the justice of God's
dealing with men in the actual course of human experience illustrates an observation of Charles S. McCoy (65, 366): 'Starting with the Eternal Decree of predestination, the Reformed scholastics deduced their theological systems. This

All this follows from trying to justify the ways of God with the reprobate. 'But, I say, there is no congruous opposition between salvation and damnation . . .'; the one must be as arbitrary as the other. For Twisse the idea of grace has been absorbed so completely into the postulate of predestination that his test of orthodoxy 'in the doctrine of Election' is willingness on all occasions to come out frankly and say that damnation is an act of God's free grace.

Twisse's captious argument makes a useful negative gloss on Cotton's statements: it shows plainly what they cannot mean and why. By distinguishing between preterition and positive condemnation Cotton cannot be trying to deny that the one purpose implies the other as well in God's secret counsels. When they are transposed into the terms in which God's secret will is revealed in time, however, the one purpose does not presuppose any condition as part of its definition, while the other does. 'For condemnation', as Cotton says, 'is an act of justice, and presupposeth a rule of justice transgressed, and thereby wrath, or just revenge provoked.'[41] The condition of being condemned has reference by definition to a prior condition, which it follows in the logical order or conditions by which God has covenanted to unfold his secret purposes. Exactly as Twisse says, 'God hath ordained that no man shall be condemned, but for sin.' No such prior condition is implied in the very idea of preterition, and so the distinction between the two aspects of God's dealing with the reprobate is at least not logically meaningless. What makes the distinction worth making, however, is that it does allow a 'congruous opposition' to appear between the just damnation of the reprobate and salvation by grace.

The process of salvation begins without prior conditions. That means for Cotton not only that the salvation of the elect was determined arbitrarily in God's secret counsels before the world began, but also that grace enters abruptly into the ordered course of ordinary conditions by which God's will is unfolded in the world. In the secret counsels of God both reprobation and salva-

strong emphasis on the single act of Divine will before creation tends to render meaningless the interaction between God and man described in Scripture and to weaken, if not destroy, the significance of history and of salvation through historical events.'

[41] 113, 42–3.

tion are absolute, but in the course of history and human experience the one is just, the other gratuitous.

The condition of grace is unique. That the day and the night succeed each other regularly can be called the 'condition' by which they exist. The whole fabric of nature can be described as consisting of conditions established by God and indicative of the relation of all things to God. Order is thus not immanent in the world, but consists of God's covenantal revelation of his will with respect to all his creatures. Man can therefore trust the underlying order of temporal experience, but not presume upon it. Its very sureness teaches him to look to his own covenantal relation with God, and only to that, as the basis of his being; fallen man, however, must find himself condemned by the condition of that Covenant but for the supervention of saving grace, which is the only condition not implied in the whole order of conditions but entering into it in mid course, so that it is wholly new.

When grace has once entered the course of human experience, however, the new condition which it creates is connected to subsequent conditions. It is gratuitous but not inconsequential. To define the Covenant of Grace as an absolute promise entailing subsequent conditions is a way of saying that the experience of grace is both unique and integral to the rest of experience. This conception of the Covenant provides an argument against Antinomianism which goes beyond the crude and dubious charge of licentiousness. The more cogent objection to the Antinomian account of Christian experience is that it seems to dissociate saving faith from all other relations of life. Merely to say that the believer is enabled or even compelled to do good works by grace following upon his faith does not heal that breach; it only amounts to an arbitrary assertion that there is some connection between faith and morality, and suggests an essentially mechanical idea of how it must work. Federal Theology offers a clear alternative account of the relation of the 'new creature' to created order.

'It is true indeed,' says Cotton, 'God worketh all things after the counsel of his will; but that proveth not that God carrieth all things with an absolute and unconditional decree of providence.'[42] Miracles are rare; God's ordinary way of effecting his purposes with respect to his creatures is according to the conditions of the Covenants which relate them to him. Man responds to his condition

[42] 113, 246.

in a different manner from the day and the night or the fowls and the beasts, however, and is thus responsible in a special way. His very consciousness of God's faithfulness in keeping covenants evokes the sense of a duty in himself to be faithful in return. This sense of responsibility is related to the prudence which obeys the laws of nature simply in order to avoid being hurt; doubtless it is also related to the 'mercenary morality' which looks for life in exchange for prescribed works; but it is a more fundamental principle than either. Far from being nullified by conversion, this fundamental sense of responsibility to God is only understood clearly in the light of the Gospel, for only then is it disentangled from considerations of prudence or the acquisition of merit. The experience of grace is not an isolated flash or a strange detachment from the conditions of temporal life; it is the realization of an entirely new condition involving all the others.

The doctrinal difference between Cotton and Twisse, then, even supposing it is more than a figment of Twisse's argumentative eagerness, does not concern their basic understanding of the Covenant of Grace as a conditional one. Nor does there appear to be any specifically doctrinal difference on this point between Cotton and such an emphatically moral preacher as Bulkeley. As has been seen, Bulkeley, like Preston, makes use of the appealing argument that the condition required in the Covenant of Grace is only a 'small' one. That argument is specious if it is taken as a definitive principle of doctrine, but the preacher who makes use of it for the purpose of inviting people to faith does not necessarily take it as definitive. Bulkeley follows it with another, more basic account of the conditionality of the Covenant:

And look in what series and order God did purpose to communicate the blessings of grace to his Elect, so as one shall succeed and follow the other, the same doth he make known in his promise, and so doth also execute and fulfill; first calling, then justifying, then glorifying, etc. *Ro.* 8.28,29,30. He doth not save till he call and justify; but first he calls to faith, and justifies, and then glorifieth him that believeth: And here though the giving of life to him that believeth be conditional and follow the giving of faith, yet is the giving of life as free grace as the giving of faith, both one and other springing from the same fountain, even from the purpose of his grace, by which he purposeth first to call unto faith, and then by faith to bring unto life and salvation. . . .

Here there is no question of man's power in himself to fulfill even such a 'small condition' as thankful acceptance of the 'royal reward'. Even that condition derives from the purpose of God's grace. The Covenant of Grace is conditional in no other sense than that the conditions springing from God's gracious purpose are communicated in a certain 'series and order'—

... so that the adding of a condition doth not abrogate the freeness of grace promised, but only shows in what order and way we must expect the blessing, one blessing of the Covenant of life going before, another following; the former being conditions to the latter, faith a condition of salvation; but both faith and salvation springing from the same purpose of grace.[43]

For the purpose of exhorting the elect to set out on their destined way, the preacher may put the same doctrine in a slightly different manner:

First, ... there is a condition of the Covenant: The Lord doth not absolutely promise life unto any; he doth not say to any soul, I will save you and bring you to life, though you continue impenitent and unbelieving; but commands and works us to repent and believe, and then promises that in the way of faith and repentance he will save us. He prescribes a way of life for us to walk in, that so we may obtain the

---

[43] 14, Sig. Ccc2. Cf. *Institutes*, III, xiv, 21 (15, 787):

The fact that Scripture shows that the good works of believers are reasons why the Lord benefits them is to be so understood as to allow what we have set forth before to stand unshaken: that the efficient cause of our salvation consists in God the Father's love; the material cause in God the Son's obedience; the instrumental cause in the Spirit's illumination, that is, faith; the final cause, in the glory of God's great generosity. These do not prevent the Lord from embracing works as inferior causes. But how does this come about? Those whom the Lord has destined by his mercy for the inheritance of eternal life he leads into possession of it, according to his ordinary dispensation, by means of good works. What goes before in the order of dispensation he calls the cause of what comes after. In this way he sometimes derives eternal life from works, not intending it to be ascribed to them; but because he justifies those whom he has chosen in order at last to glorify them, he makes the prior grace, which is a step to that which follows, as it were the cause.

Cf. also Jonathan Edwards' remark, 'There is a difference between being justified by a thing, and that thing universally, and necessarily, and inseparably attending or going with justification.' Perry Miller quotes this as showing that Edwards 'went to physics for a cause that does not bind the effect by producing it; he found in the new science (few besides Newton himself understood that this was the hidden meaning of the *Principia*) the concept of an antecedent to a subsequent, in which the subsequent, when it does come to pass, proves to be whatever it is by itself and in itself, without determination by the precedent' (70, 78–9). Whether or not Edwards detected such a hidden meaning in Newton, he could easily find the idea plainly stated in the Covenant Theologians and in Calvin. See also 25, 64–5.

salvation which he hath promised; he brings us first through the door of faith, *Act.* 14. And then he carries us on in the way of faith, till he bring us to the end of our faith, the salvation of our souls.[44]

The preacher begins by evoking that sense of human responsibility which he can only express by insisting that 'there is a condition of the Covenant.' Then, with 'commands and works us', he prepares to modulate to the unconditional key, so to speak, and by the end of the passage he is describing the condition of the faithful in terms which, quoted out of context, might almost seem quietist. Well aware of this danger, however, a preacher like Bulkeley (or Richard Senhouse or Robert Browne) will always take pains to say 'commands us', often leaving 'and works us' to be understood.

Another consideration may prompt the preacher to go further and speak as though the Covenant of Grace put man in a position actually to force God's hand. One of the most basic complaints of the Reformation is that the Roman Church's system of penance keeps believers in a perpetual state of anxiety about their sins, depriving them of that underlying peace of conscience which should come from reconciliation with God by Christ's propitiation. 'But if it is a question of quieting the conscience,' Calvin asks, 'what will this quieting be if a man hears that sins are redeemed by satisfactions? When can he at length be certain of the measure of that satisfaction? Then he will always doubt whether he has a merciful God; he will always be troubled, and always tremble.'[45] Preachers like Richard Sibbes are persuaded, in fact, that papists have an interest in keeping poor souls in such a state:

And further, to lay open offenders in this kind, what spirit shall we think them to be of, that take advantage of the bruisedness and infirmities of men's spirits to relieve them with false peace for their own worldly ends? A wounded spirit will part with anything. Most of the gainful points of popery, as confession, satisfaction, merit, purgatory, etc., spring from hence, but they are physicians of no value, or rather tormenters than physicians at all.[46]

The Reformers therefore insist that anyone who has been truly called can be absolutely sure that 'he has a merciful God' precisely because God's purpose of election is absolute:

Wherefore thou must not doubt of thy salvation, by reason of thy daily slips, proceeding from thy weakness of faith, no not for heinous

[44] 14, Sig. (Ss4).   [45] 15, 653–4, III, iv, 27.   [46] 108, I, 62.

crimes: like as neither David for his adultery and murder, nor Peter for his threefold denial, did despair of their election: which appeareth, in that being plunged in the very gulfs of their temptations, they held fast their faith as an anchor, and called upon God.... Lastly, in no wise must we forget, namely that our election is certain and immutable: and therefore, as it is done without respect of any works of ours: so in like sort it can never be changed by any of our evil deserts. For as it first proceeded from the only free purpose of God: so it is grounded thereon. True it is, we provoke God's wrath against us by our sins, and neither will God let them escape unpunished, but he chastiseth us by diverse, both inward and outward scourges: as may appear in David above all other.[47]

If the Reformation gives special emphasis to the unaccountable sovereignty of God, it also emphasizes anew the invitation 'to come boldly unto the throne of grace' (Heb. 4:16), and the terminology of the Covenant lends itself aptly to this purpose. It is 'a boldness God likes well enough', says Richard Senhouse, 'to press him with his promises; that hath God said it, and shall he not do it? hath he spoken it, and hath he not accomplished it?'[48] The greatest blessing of the Covenant of Grace in this mortal life, Bulkeley affirms, is that it 'doth settle the soul in peace' as the other covenant can never do:

The covenant of works rested in, and trusted unto, can never (in this state of corruption that we are now in) work settled comfort, peace, and quietness of heart. Let a man walk as exactly as flesh and blood can attain unto, and let him (withal) build as confidently on this foundation as he possibly may, yet the heart will be still in suspicion, in doubt, in fear, uncertain what to trust unto, doubtful what his estate is. But the covenant of grace rested in, and trusted unto, doth settle the soul in peace.[49]

'For comfort unto such as see their own unworthiness, and are discouraged thereby from seeking after grace with God', they can be told to

plead before the throne of grace. There bring out the words of the Testament, and say, *Lord, here is thine own Covenant and promise*; hold the Lord fast to his promise which he hath made, and plead with him, and say, Lord, why are thy mercies restrained from me? Where is thy

---

[47] 86, 34.
[48] 107, Sig. C3.
[49] 14, Sig. (O4)ᵛ–P(1).

faithfulness? Why dost not thou pardon mine iniquity? Though I be worthy to perish, yet remember thy Covenant, make good thy promise, in which thou hast caused thy servant to trust. Such importunity the Lord will not take ill. He delights thus to be overcome by the pleas of his people.[50]

It is 'no arrogancy but faith,' says John Downame, 'to show what thou hast received; it is not pride but devotion.'[51]

By a slight shift of approach, this argument of 'Consolation to the weak Saints of God, who are often cast down in themselves, through sense of their own infirmities'[52] can be turned into a means of combating infirmities. To the poor soul who doubts 'of keeping Covenant on my part', Preston answers:

> *Beloved*, . . . thou needest not fear that thy disobedience, if thou be once within the Covenant (if thou be one whose heart is *upright* with him), shall cause the *Lord* to depart from thee. He will not be unfaithful to thee, though thou be weak in thy carriage to him: *for he keeps covenant forever*. That is, his Covenant is to keep thy heart in his fear, that thing we forget. If the *Lord* keep Covenant with us, he doth not suspend his promise upon our obedience, and leave us so; but he promiseth to give us a heart and a spirit to serve him. . . .[53]

Preston's comfort to the 'weak Saints' is that their disobedience will not keep God from helping them to be obedient. Because God will never give them up, they must never give up. If they find they cannot fulfill some condition of the Covenant, they can count on Christ to enable them:

> And so . . . put the case thou know *God*, thou seest him in his attributes, thou hearest him often described, and art able to describe him to others, but for all this, thou findest not thy heart affectioned toward him, . . . thou canst not say thou lovest him *with all thy heart, with all thy soul, and with all thy strength*. What wilt thou do in this case? Go to *Christ*, the Prophet, and beseech him that he would teach thee to know the LORD, this is his promise; if thou pray to him, and he do not do it, urge him with this, it is a part of his *Covenant*, that he hath confirmed by Oath, and must do it; and be assured of this, if we seek, and be earnest with him, he will teach us to know the *Lord*, and to know

---

[50] 14, Sig. N2^v.
[51] 34, 263.
[52] 14, Sig. O(1)^v.
[53] 91, 91.

him so, that we shall love him with all our soul, and with all our strength. The like may I say of any thing else.[54]

It may be a strange way to go about loving, but it follows logically from the conditionality of the Covenant. Because God will always do his part in the Covenant, you can be confident of doing yours.

If you are in the Covenant, then, you will certainly perform the conditions of the Covenant. Conversely, if you perform the conditions you must be in the Covenant. By its conditional nature the Covenant of Grace neatly supports the argument of the first Epistle of John with respect to what William Perkins calls the greatest 'Case of Conscience . . . that ever was: How a man may know whether he be the Child of God, or no'.[55] Once grace has entered the course of life it produces conditions in a regular 'series and order'. Therefore it should be possible to trace the series back to verify the original condition. John Downame explains that although

the sanctification which is an inseparable fruit and effect of God's election in all his children . . . be the last in nature and next to salvation itself, for first God electeth, & whom he calleth those he justifieth, and lastly, whom he justifieth those he sanctifieth and saveth; yet when we are to gather assurance of our election, we are not to observe this order, but to begin where the Lord endeth, and so ascend from the lowest degree till we come to the highest.[56]

Thus, as George Downame puts it, 'the conditions of the Covenant are the bottom ground, not of salvation, but of our evidence of interest in salvation.'[57] Salvation itself is still 'upon a free bottom', but in Thomas Blake's words, 'Assurance of salvation cannot be gained, but in a way of Covenant-keeping; yea, the conditions of the Covenant are the basis and never-failing bottom of our Evidence and Assurance.'[58]

Thus while the sense in which the Covenant of Grace is absolute allows the preacher to reassure the souls under his tutelage, the sense in which it is conditional allows him still to use the good old anxieties for all they are worth:

Now what stronger bridle to curb in our unruly flesh, when it is ready to run into sin, than to be assured that if we live in sin, and fulfill our carnal lusts, we are in the state of condemnation? What sharper spur to

---

[54] 91, 376–7.   [55] 87.   [56] 34, 231.   [57] 35, 151.   [58] 8, 150.

prick us forward when we are ready to faint, or slack our pace in the Christian race of holiness and righteousness, than to consider that our sanctification and newness of life is the only means whereby we may come to the assurance of our election and salvation?[59]

If the sight of their infirmities makes the 'weak Saints' doubt their election, they are to renew their assurance by performing works of sanctification. The conditionality of the Covenant of Grace allows sound Protestant preachers to use 'the bruisedness and infirmities of men's spirits', if not 'for their own worldly ends' precisely, yet for the sake of good order in the world.

If the Roman Church provides fearful souls with a system of palpable satisfactions and merits, the doctrine of Covenant conditions induces a similar dependence on secular good works. Good works even take on a quasi-sacramental function as 'seals' of the Covenant. Thomas Blake argues:

I know some finding in Scripture, the seal of the Spirit, and the witness of the Spirit in order to Assurance, will have the whole of the work of Assurance to be carried on alone by the Spirit, that all is done in us without us, a secret whisper from God, that we are God's, and no more. This must be heeded, and our faith or repentance in the work not at all regarded; but I would know of those, if the Spirit be a seal, whether the soul doth not bear the impress? and what this impress is, but the graces of the Spirit? The Seal sealing, and the impress made fully answer one the other. Sometimes it may dimly answer, where the wax or clay, or whatsoever is sealed, takes not a full impression; but if it answer not, it is no Seal. The graces that the Spirit works are its impress, and these are the conditions of the Covenant. . . .[60]

It is in just this sense of an impress such as that affixed to a document, as opposed to the sense of a 'Seal sealing', that the sacraments are called 'seals'. As the outward and visible signs of inward graces, good works become, as it were, the sacramental elements. John Downame describes them in phrases which recall the commonplace argument against reducing the sacraments to 'bare signs':

Neither are these effects bare signs only of our election, but also manifest seals which by their plain impression do evidently assure us thereof: so that though we do not directly and immediately know God's election, predestination, & decreeing that we shall be saved, yet we may plainly see apparent seals and impressions hereof in ourselves, lively resembling that which is secret in God's hidden counsel; and as we not seeing the seal which maketh the impression, do easily discern the form, fashion, & quantity thereof by the print which it hath made; so we not seeing God's secret decree of predestination, may notwithstanding attain to the evident knowledge thereof, by that impression which it maketh in us.[61]

The conditionality of the Covenant of Grace makes all the business of life potentially sacramental. Every good action is a seal of God's favour, for 'the effects of God's election do not only as signs signify, but also as seals confirm unto us the assurance thereof. . . .'[62] By the same token every lapse renews the need of reassurance. For the likes of Peter or David, or of young Martin Luther, the method of seeking assurance of God's favour from the evidence of one's sanctification may leave something to be desired, but for ordinary, decent folks it is good to have something tangible to refer to for assurance, even at the cost of a certain fretfulness.

By this use of the Covenant, preachers in the tradition that runs from William Tyndale through William Perkins to such men as Preston and George and John Downame are able to translate the message of salvation by faith into the strain of relentless morality which has been singled out by posterity to represent 'Puritanism'.[63] George Downame, for example, finds in Zechariah's exultant psalm of thanksgiving 'this most profitable instruction':

That seeing the oath of the Lord, whereby he promiseth to give to all them that are delivered from the hand of their spiritual enemies (that is

---

[61] 34, 255–6. Compare, for example, John Jewel's remark concerning the sacraments: 'What? Are they nothing else but bare and naked signs? God forbid. They are the seals of God, heavenly tokens, and signs of grace, and righteousness, and mercy given and imputed to us' (59, II, 1101).

[62] 34, 227–8.

[63] William A. Clebsh (20) argues for the filiation of English Puritanism to the early Tudor Reformers, especially Tyndale, disputing Leonard J. Trinterud's thesis (112) that it owes its origins to the influence of the Rhineland theologians. Tyndale's kind of religion may have been more prevalent in the early period of Puritanism than the writings of such men as Robert Crowley, Anthony Gilby, Walter Travers, and Thomas Cartwright would seem to indicate, since the topics of the vestiarian and Admonition controversies give little occasion for it to appear. However, it is only with such men as William Perkins that it clearly begins to emerge as the dominant type of Puritanism. (For other objections to Trinterud's thesis see New (79, 91–4), although New misapplies the first statement he quotes from Calvin in this connection.)

to all that are redeemed by CHRIST) grace to worship him in holiness &
righteousness, is infallible, we should therefore be careful to bring forth
these fruits of our redemption; otherwise we can have no assurance that
we are redeemed of the LORD.[64]

Regarded from this angle all the promises of grace become reasons
to be 'careful'. The 'good news' of Christianity gives new force to
all the old 'admonitions and comminations', in John Downame's
phrase, directed to 'hypocrites and secure worldlings' who need to
be 'roused out of their security', but also to the faithful, 'who may
and ought to be assured of their election' by their response. If the
effect on the faithful is sometimes hard to distinguish from the
terror prescribed for worldlings, that too is all to the good; for 'the
dear children of God', so long as they are in this life, are 'partly
flesh and partly spirit':

. . . therefore as they have need that the spiritual man should be comforted and their faith confirmed against diffidence and doubting, with
the sweet promises of the Gospel; so had they need to have their unruly
flesh curbed in, and restrained from falling into retchless security, by
these admonitions and comminations. . . . Therefore that we may keep
the strait way without declining on either hand, God doth as it were
hedge us in on both sides, to restrain us from wandering; on the one
side with sweet promises, that we may not despair, but rely ourselves
on his strength and assistance; on the other side with strict admonitions
and fearful comminations, that we may not trust too much unto our
own power, nor presume upon our own abilities: and by the means of
the one, he doth as it were prick us forward in our journey, keeping us
from once thinking of standing still, or returning again into Egypt; and
by the other as with an hand he doth uphold us, when we are weary and
ready to faint, having an eye to the crown of glory, and the garland of
happiness, which is prepared for us at the end of our course, and race
of Christianity.[65]

On the one side the blessing, on the other side the curse. Paul's
argument from the Covenant had always contained the unrecog-
nized possibility of a new Deuteronomy, its essential faith in the
God of Abraham cleared from ceremonial requirements, and its
hope projected into a promised life to come.

To produce this unlooked-for result from Paul's argument
against Judaizing it is only necessary to obscure the central figure

---

[64] 35, 10.
[65] 34, 249–50.

in all of Paul's thought, 'Jesus Christ, and him crucified'. To be sure, there is a place for Christ in the Federal Theology. An important difference between the Covenant of Works and the Covenant of Grace is, as Thomas Blake says,

That the first Covenant between God and man was immediate, no Mediator intervening, no days-man standing between them to make them one; but for the second, man being fallen by sin, a Mediator was necessary, that God and man now in that distance, should be reconciled.[66]

Because fallen man was in no condition to negotiate with God, the Covenant of Grace was originally transacted between God the Father and God the Son, as Bulkeley explains:

That there is a covenant passed betwixt the Father and the Son, concerning our salvation, I willingly grant, and shall open and confirm by Scripture. The whole business of our salvation was first transacted between the Father and Christ, before it was revealed to us; hence we are said to be given to Christ, *Joh.* 17.6.10., as if the Father should say to the Son, 'These I take to be vessels of mercy, and these thou shalt bring unto me, for they will destroy themselves, but thou shalt save them out of their lost estate'; and then the Son taketh them at his Father's hand, and looking at his Father's will (*Joh.* 6.37.39), he taketh care that none be lost of them which his Father hath given him.[67]

But the very fact that Christ's mediating role can be so satisfactorily accounted for in terms of the Covenant tends to reduce it to a formality. Neither the human person of Jesus nor the incarnate Logos nor the mystery of participation in the death and resurrection of Christ is a theme of lively interest in the Federal Theology. Bulkeley can 'willingly grant' the need of a mediator in the Covenant of Grace, but it is really to the Covenant itself that he looks for salvation. The Covenant itself is the real mediator between God's secret election and its objects.

It is here that the Federal Theology diverges most significantly from the emphasis of Calvin's teaching. 'Indeed, it is true that faith looks to one God', Calvin says:

But this must also be added, 'To know Jesus Christ whom he has sent.' For God would have remained hidden afar off if Christ's splendor had

---

[66] 8, 13.
[67] 14, 31.

not beamed upon us. For this purpose the Father laid up with his only-begotten Son all that he had to reveal himself in Christ, so that Christ, by communicating his Father's benefits, might express the true image of his glory. It has been said that we must be drawn by the Spirit to be aroused to seek Christ; so, in turn, we must be warned that the invisible Father is to be sought solely in this image.[68]

By contrast, Preston illustrates how the fervour and indeed some of the very phrases which have formerly been devoted to Christ can be transferred to the abstract idea of the Covenant:

My beloved, it is the greatest point that ever we had yet opportunity to deliver to you; yea, it is the main point that the Ministers of the Gospel can deliver at any time, neither can they deliver a point of greater moment, nor can you hear any, than the description of the Covenant of Grace: this is that you must lay up for the foundation of all your comforts: it hath been the corner stone upon which the Saints have been built, from the beginning of the world, unto this day: there is no ground you have to believe you shall be saved, there is no ground to believe that any promise of *God* shall be made good to you, to believe that you shall have the price of the high calling of *God* in *Jesus Christ*, and those glorious riches of the inheritance prepared for us in him; I say, there is no other ground at all, but upon this Covenant; all that we teach you, from day to day, are but conclusions drawn from this Covenant; they are all built upon this: therefore, if ever you had cause to attend anything, you have reason to attend to this; I say, this Covenant between GOD and us.[69]

Despite the vestigial formula 'in *Jesus Christ*', this faith has Jesus no more clearly in view than Abraham's can have done. It is a simple and immediate trust in the all-sufficiency of God and in 'this Covenant between GOD and us':

. . . for let a man believe that *God is All-sufficient*, which is the *Covenant*, for *justifying faith* is but a believing of that part of the *Covenant*, and enabling a man to keep the other part which is required; and, I say, it makes a man *righteous*. . . . It knits his heart unto the *Lord*. It *sanctifieth*

---

[68] 15, 543–4: III, ii, 1.

[69] 91, 350–1. Preston is surely recalling the repeated scriptural description of Christ as the 'corner stone' or 'foundation': Matt. 21:42, Mark 12:10, Luke 20:17, Acts 4:11, 1 Cor. 3:11, Eph. 2:21, 1 Pet. 2:6. He may have in mind the usage of Isaiah ('I the Lord have called thee in righteousness, and will hold thine hand, and will keep thee, and give thee for a covenant of the people, for a light of the Gentiles' (42:6; cf. 49:8)) as a warrant for identifying Christ with the Covenant, so as to use the same phrases to refer to either.

a man *throughout*, it makes him *peculiar* to the *Lord*, it makes him *wholly* to him. This is the nature of *faith*.[70]

The Federal Theology tends to make the formal structure of Trinitarian orthodoxy serve as the vehicle of an essentially monarchian religion.

Cotton resists this tendency of the Federal Theology. In order to direct the faith of Christians clearly to Christ, he mounts a quiet but radical attack on what has been described here as the quasi-sacramental function of covenant conditions. Nobody in Cotton's part of the world would object to Calvin's warning that 'assurance of salvation does not depend upon participation in the sacrament, as if justification consisted in it. For we know that justification is lodged in Christ alone';[71] but Cotton's warning, 'take heed you do not close with promises before we have Jesus Christ in them: especially take heed you make not use of a promise to a gracious qualification, to give you your part in Christ',[72] caused 'as much Agitation as any other Doctrine that is taught among us'.[73] Cotton's attack on the 'Doctrine of Marks and Signs',[74] as he calls it, reawakens the first impulses of the Reformation.

The distinction between Cotton's teaching on this point and that of the dominant school of Puritanism does not concern the question whether the Covenant is absolute or conditional; as has been seen, all parties agree that it is both, even though they differ in their predilection for the one or the other aspect of it. Nor is there any question whether the performance of Covenant conditions conveys assurance *ex opere operato*, so to speak; all would subscribe to Cotton's condemnation of those who 'are so clouded with fears of their estates, that if they come to be assured of God's love, they will a while love good duties, but afterward fall back again to a customary performance, and rest themselves contented with the deed done.'[75] Deeds are only as good as the condition of faith from which they follow, and as Preston says, 'It much concerns us, to know whether they be right or counterfeit.'[76] 'I do not know any of all the Teachers in the Country', Cotton can assert,

that withdraw their consents from this doctrine, that such Sanctification as is wrought in Hypocrites, though it may reach to great improvements,

---

[70] 91, 13.　　[71] 15, 1290: IV, xiv, 14.　　[72] 26, 103.　　[73] 26, 58.
[74] 24, 35.　　[75] 23, 5.　　[76] 91, 2.

10—P.R.I.E.

yet it is no evidence of Justification at all, And it hath been handled in another Congregation, and I think not without weight of truth, that to distinguish in men between that Sanctification which floweth from the Law, and that which is of the Gospel, is a matter so narrow, that the Angels in Heaven have much ado to discern who differ. . . .[77]

The dominant school of Puritan preaching responds to this difficulty by urging Christians 'to descend into themselves, & to examine how it is with them *within* . . .'.[78] The 'Doctrine of Marks and Signs' leads to an exacting introspection such as Bulkeley describes:

Seeing God's end in the Covenant of grace is to glorify his grace in us, we may by this in some measure discern what part we have in the grace of this Covenant. And we may do it by this, if *our* aims and *God's* aims, our ends and God's ends meet in one, when we come to seek grace in his sight. Many an one comes before God, begs mercy, and yet obtains it not; as *Pro.* 1.28. because they ask amiss, they seek it not in God's way. Consider therefore, what seekest thou in begging mercy at his hand? Dost thou seek only to have thy sin pardoned? *only* to be saved from wrath? This will not argue thy peace, that thou art under grace. But dost thou as well seek the glorifying of his grace towards thee, as the obtaining of thine own peace with him? If God hath put this disposition of heart into thee, that thou couldest be content to lie down in the dust, and to take shame for thy sin before Angels and men, so that the abundant riches of his grace may be glorified in the taking away of thy sin, if thy desire be not only that thou maist see his salvation, but that the Lord himself may be made marvelous, and his grace magnified in thee, then thou art herein another *David*, a man after God's own heart, thy thoughts are as God's thoughts, therefore as a pledge of his grace towards thee. Never couldest thou so desire the glorifying of that grace, if God had not a purpose of grace towards thee.[79]

The preacher appeals to an anxious self-interest to motivate an intense self-scrutiny, to which he promises the reward of assurance if it reveals a motive that is not self-centred. This passage epitomizes the difficulty inherent in the strategy of urging men to search themselves for those very conditions of the Covenant of Grace which, as has been said, 'carry man out of himself' (8, 72). It is like straining every nerve in an effort to relax—'labour to get humiliation', Preston urges.[80]

[77] 26, 59.
[78] 14, Sig. Vv2^v.
[79] 14, Sig. N2–N2^v.
[80] 92, 298.

Cotton is simply teaching the same doctrine by a strategy more consistent with it when he warns that the soul of natural man

... will always think that he can do something; and is not able to come out of himself to utter denial of himself, even all his own gifts, and parts, and good works whatsoever; for a man is never utterly denied, until there be nothing left of which a man can say, This I am able to do, or this is an hopeful thing in me; and when it cometh to this pass, then will the soul lie down at the will of God and acknowledge that if the Lord would never show him mercy, just and righteous are his judgments.[81]

The basic difference between Cotton and such a preacher as Bulkeley is that Cotton does not conclude from the ambiguity of marks and signs that men must 'descend into themselves' in quest of assurance, but uses that ambiguity as an argument against putting trust in any 'hopeful thing' that man may find in himself. Instead of pursuing the 'Doctrine of Marks and Signs' into the labyrinth of the heart, Cotton simply warns, 'Trust not ... upon every leaning of your soul upon conditional promises. . . .'[82]

Precisely because the conditions of the Covenant of Grace enter into the whole fabric of conditions whereby God effects his manifold purposes in the world, they are unsure supports for the soul. This is as true of inward conditions as of outward works. Even genuine inspiration by the Spirit of God is no sure sign of saving faith, for 'You know what was said of *Saul*, I Sam. 10.10. *The Spirit of God came upon him*, and so did it likewise upon *Judas* and *Demas*, acting them mightily in their Administrations. . . .'[83] They were 'carried along by the Spirit' to serve God's good purposes, yet were themselves vessels of wrath. Cotton rehearses in a new context Calvin's arguments to the effect that 'nothing prevents God from illumining some with a momentary awareness of his grace, which afterward vanishes.'[84] He follows Calvin closely also in arguing that even the single-minded commitment to God which can be evoked from the Old Testament is not to be trusted as a sign of saving faith. 'I admit', Calvin says, '. . . that God's truth is, as they call it, the common object of faith, whether he threaten or

[81] 26, 187.
[82] 26, 104.
[83] 26, 61.
[84] 15, 556: III, ii, 11.

hold out hope of grace', but that is only one aspect of faith, and it is not the aspect 'which separates believers from unbelievers':

We seek a faith that distinguishes the children of God from the wicked, and believers from unbelievers. If someone believes that God both justly commands all that he commands and truly threatens, shall he therefore be called a believer? By no means! Therefore, there can be no firm condition of faith unless it rests upon God's mercy. Now, what is our purpose in discussing faith? Is it not that we may grasp the way of salvation? But how can there be saving faith except in so far as it engrafts us in the body of Christ?[85]

The very fact that 'admonitions and comminations' have an effect on the unregenerate shows that the unregenerate have a kind of faith; and as Cotton points out, it is not necessarily devoid of inward comfort:

... the spirit of bondage will marvelously prevail with the Sons of men to draw them on to strong works of Reformation, from whence they reap no small Consolation, but think and say (as *Abijah* did) that *the Lord is with them whilst they are with him*: And as sometimes *David* said of himself, *I believed, therefore I spake*, so the *Israelites* also (*Psal.* 106.12.) *believed and sang the praises of the Lord upon the red sea shore,* and yet were they but an Hypocritical Generation ...[86]

That very 'Act of faith, which is a staying a man's self upon God' cannot be relied on as a sign, for 'what saith the Text, *Isa.* 48.2. *They stay themselves upon the God of Israel*; and these were obstinate sinners, and their neck as an iron sinew, and their brow as brass. ...'[87] Paradoxically, man cannot put his faith in faith itself: 'As for faith of the Gospel of Jesus Christ, it is never prefident of its own power, but his strength lieth out of himself in Christ; whereas hypocrites and legal Christians are confident of their faith. ...'[88] Hypocrites and 'legal Christians' can very well find comfort and 'refreshing in their way and work' in

... a Covenant, in which the Voice of the Lord is, *If you be true and faithful to me, then I will not remove you*, and in this Covenant is Faith found, whereby they lay hold upon the head of the Sacrifice, but not on Christ: it is only built upon such changes as they find in themselves, and will in the end vanish utterly away.[89]

---

[85] 15, 556: III, ii, 30.
[86] 26, 62.
[87] 26, 64.
[88] 26, 65–6.
[89] 26, 42.

By such arguments Cotton renounces from the outset the whole casuistry of religious affections which characterizes the last phase of Puritanism.

Yet Bulkeley distorts Cotton's argument when he says that 'the meaning of those that oppose this way of evidencing by our sanctification, is to remove all evidence by anything in ourselves, whether by faith, or any other Grace, and to urge only the immediate revelation of the Spirit....'[90] Cotton does not 'remove' the evidence of sanctification but warns against dwelling upon it. The evidence can be valid *a posteriore*[91] so long as the believer does not turn to it as his source of hope. Nor does Cotton's rejection of the 'Doctrine of Marks and Signs' throw believers back on the 'immediate revelation of the Spirit' in any other sense than that in which the Protestant attitude toward the sacraments can also be said to do so. Cotton only insists, as did the first Reformers, that the Spirit which is communicated in Christ by the word of the Gospel is not tied to the elements of the world.

But if 'this mediate witness of the Spirit which is by habitual and inherent graces, is not to be harkened unto, until the immediate witness hath spoken',[92] Bulkeley sees mankind as helplessly confronting the hidden God:

Would we then know whether we be of the number of those that are saved by the blood of the Covenant? We need not for this ascend up into heaven, to search the book of God's election, nor need we go down into the lower parts of the earth, for any there to tell us that we are delivered thence; but go down into our own hearts, and if we find this work of sanctification there wrought, then what *Moses* said of *Israel, Blessed art thou O Israel, a people saved by the Lord*, the same may be truly said of us; Our salvation is begun, we have the seal of it, the earnest, the first fruits, which shall at length bring the full possession of the whole harvest....[93]

---

[90] 14, Sig. (Mm3)ᵛ.

[91] 'And if ever the Lord minister comfort unto any man, true comfort upon good grounds is ever built upon a Promise of free grace. If the witness be unto Justification received, it is true indeed, a gracious Qualification, and a Promise to it, may give good Evidence of it *a posteriore*' (26, 57).

[92] 14, Sig. Mm1ᵛ.

[93] 14, Sig. (Mm3)ᵛ. Arguing against those who 'make election depend upon faith, as if it were doubtful and also ineffectual until confirmed by faith', Calvin says, 'Indeed, that it is confirmed, with respect to us, is so utterly plain; we have also already seen that the secret plan of God which lay hidden, is brought to

Bulkeley's phrases recall Romans 10:5–11, where Paul turns the words of Deuteronomy into a description of the way of salvation by faith. Deuteronomy says that the commandment of God

... is not hidden from thee, neither is it far off. It is not in heaven, that thou shouldest say, Who shall go up for us to heaven, and bring it unto us, that we may hear it, and do it? Neither is it beyond the sea, that thou shouldest say, Who shall go over the sea for us, and bring it unto us, that we may hear it, and do it? (30.11–13.)

Paul makes these words refer to Christ:

For Moses describeth the righteousness which is of the law, That the man which doeth those things shall live by them. But the righteousness which is of faith speaketh on this wise, Say not in thine heart, Who shall ascend into heaven? (that is, to bring Christ down from above:) Or, Who shall descend into the deep? (that is, to bring up Christ again from the dead.)

Thus where Deuteronomy concludes, 'But the word is very nigh unto thee, in thy mouth, and in thy heart, that thou mayest do it', Paul says, rather,

The word is nigh thee, even in thy mouth, and in thy heart: that is, the word of faith, which we preach; That if thou shalt confess with thy mouth the Lord Jesus, and shalt believe in thine heart that God hath raised him from the dead, thou shalt be saved.

light, provided you understand by this language merely that what was unknown is now verified—sealed, as it were, with a seal.' This leads him to an observation which Bulkeley may have been recalling: 'In the meantime, I do not deny that to be assured of our salvation we must begin with the Word, and that our confidence ought to be so intent as to call upon God as our Father. For some men, to make sure about God's plan, which is near us, in our mouth and heart, perversely yearn to flit about above the clouds. This rashness, therefore, must be restrained by the soberness of faith that in his outward Word, God may sufficiently witness his secret grace to us. . . . Therefore, as it is wrong to make the force of election contingent upon faith in the gospel, by which we feel that it appertains to us, so we shall be following the best order if, in seeking the certainty of our election, we cling to those latter signs which are sure attestations of it' (15, 968: III, xxiv, 3–4). Although this passage shows how the 'Doctrine of Marks and Signs' can be plausibly derived from Calvin, it does not show him teaching it. It is not works of sanctification that he refers to as 'those latter signs', but the meaning of the word to the believer, and like Cotton he concludes: 'Christ, then, is the mirror wherein we must, and without self-deception may, contemplate our own election. For since it is into his body the Father has destined those to be engrafted whom he has willed from eternity to be his own, that he may hold as sons all whom he acknowledges to be among his members, we have a sufficiently clear and firm testimony that we have been inscribed in the book of life if we are in communion with Christ' (15, 970: III, xxiv, 5).

For Bulkeley this means that man should look into his own heart for evidence of salvation; and where Paul substituted Christ for the commandment, Bulkeley in turn leaves out Christ and speaks of the 'work of sanctification' wrought in our hearts, which is to be measured by the commandment. By substituting the assurance of salvation for salvation itself as the object of the quest, and the conditions of the Covenant for Christ as the effective means of mediation between God and man, the Federal Theology tends to undo Paul's transformation of Deuteronomy.

Against this tendency Cotton uses every argument at his disposal to show that

This is the true rest of the soul when it groweth up in a lively Faith in Jesus Christ, and yet resteth not in this, that it is sanctified, but doth look principally after Jesus Christ, and blesseth God for sanctification, making use of it for those ends for which God hath given it, but dares not rest in it as the ground of his blessedness.[94]

Again and again Cotton turns our attention away from signs and tokens of covenant conditions, whether outward or inward, and toward Christ. 'Many an Israelite stung by the fiery Serpents in the wilderness might look up to the brazen Serpent for healing,' he says, 'and yet at that time not look to their eye, nor think upon their eye by which they looked.'[95] Just so, Christians must not become so preoccupied with their faith itself that they lose sight of its object, Christ. Cotton repeats the name of Christ with the insistency of an incantation:

If the Lord Jesus Christ by his Spirit giveth us these gifts, it is our part then first to see that we do not rest in any Sanctification which doth not spring from Christ, conveyed unto us by his Spirit conveying us to him; the Spirit knitteth us unto Christ, & Christ unto us: he worketh Faith in us to receive whatsoever the Lord giveth unto us, and by the same Faith worketh all our holiness for us, I *Cor.* 1.30. *Christ is made unto us,* &c. Therefore we are to see him the principal author of all these things in us, and for us; this is the principal comfort of all gifts (Christ given in them) and the glory of all our safety; and so far as any of these lieth in our Sanctification, we ought to see that it be Sanctification in Jesus Christ; and then it is so, when the Lord giveth us to look unto the Lord Jesus in it, and to it in him; and as we look for our holiness to be perfect in *Jesus Christ*, so we look for continual supply of it from him; and this

[94] 26, 80.
[95] 28, 44.

it is to make Christ our Sanctification, when as whatsoever gift the Lord giveth us, we go not forth in the strength of it, but in the strength of Jesus Christ.[96]

This insistence on Christ as the vital centre of Christian faith sets John Cotton apart from the dominant school of Puritanism in his time and would warrant his being called 'the first consistent and authentic Calvinist in New England'.[97]

EXCURSUS

The general identification of the command to Adam with the morality of the Old Testament leads to a difficulty which William Twisse notices in his critique of Cotton. 'The covenant of works', as Bulkeley says, 'forgiveth no sin; there is nothing but strict justice in that covenant. In this Covenant, God looks not at any man's repentance and turning from sin, but only considers whether he hath sinned: . . . And hence it is, that when *Adam* had sinned, the inquisition is not whether he repented him of the evil that he had done, but, what hast thou done?' (14, Sig. N(1).) The idea of repentance is by no means foreign to the Old Law, however, and so Cotton is led to include it in the Covenant of Works:

God doth covenant and promise in the Covenant of Grace to give life to the Elect, out of his grace in Christ: so here doth God covenant and promise, in the Covenant of Works, to give life to *Adam* and all his posterity, if they continue in obedience of his Law; or if, breaking this Law, they return again to him by repentance; as it is described at large, *Gen.* 4.7. *Levit.* 18.5. *Ezek.* 18.5. & 20.11. & 40.21. *Gal.* 3.12. Surely then, the purpose of God's just retribution is to give life to the world of mankind, upon condition of their obedience, or of their repentance after disobedience (113, 62).

---

[96] 26, 150–1.

[97] 69, 98. Miller's subsequent recantation of this phrase as applied to Jonathan Edwards simply confounds confusion: 'But actually, in his substitution of the revolutionary psychology of John Locke for the medieval scheme of the faculties (which John Calvin automatically assumed), and by his replacing of the medieval physics with the new science of Sir Isaac Newton, Edwards was unable—even had he so desired—to retrieve the original positions of John Calvin. What I meant to say, and miserably spoiled in the saying, is only that Edwards brushed aside the (by his day) rusty mechanism of the covenant to forge a fresh statement of the central Protestant definition of man's plight in a universe which God created' (69, 50). For an example of what Miller means by saying that Newton made 'the original positions of John Calvin' untenable for Edwards see p. 121, n. 43, above. For a well-informed and thoughtful account of Jonathan Edwards' use of the Federal Theology, and his positions on the matters discussed in this chapter, see Conrad Cherry (19).

(None of the specific verses referred to by Cotton mentions repentence, but other verses of Ezekiel 18 and 20 do so. The reference to Ezekiel 40:21 is evidently an error.) Twisse objects:

> But what evidence, I pray, have you for this? namely, that God made any such Covenant with *Adam* in the state of innocency? who ever was found to entertain any such conceit before you? why might not you as well devise the like Covenant to be made by God with the Angels? Nay, is not the contrary manifest? *In the day thou sinnest thou shalt die the death.* How could this be verified, if God made any such Covenant with *Adam*? For, if he were under such a Covenant, he could not be said to violate it by sinning, but only by refusing to repent after he had sinned. And I verily believe you have no such meaning, as if you conceived any such Covenant to be made with *Adam* before his fall; and therefore you clapped *Adam* and his posterity together; to the end that if that which you delivered might not hold of the one, it might of the other (113, 64–5).

Indeed, repentance is itself a form of obedience, and so to frame the Covenant of Works as Cotton has done is 'to distinguish the *Genus* from the *Species*, so as to set one in opposition to the other'. Or if obedience is to be defined in such a way as to make a difference between it and repentance, then it must mean 'such a state or condition of obedience as is without all sin', and Cotton's version of the Covenant with 'the world of mankind' while they were in that state amounts to a promise of life

> ... *upon condition of their being without sin, or of their repentance after obedience.* To this I answer, That there never was any such Covenant of God with man; I mean, in such sort conditionate: and consequently, there never was any purpose in God to make any such Covenant with man; at least for the time past: As for the times to come, let them speak for themselves, by their own experience, when they come. But that never any such Covenant had place hitherto, between God and man, it is manifest; For, since the Fall of *Adam* all being born in sin, there is no place for such a Covenant, as touching the first part of the condition, which is, of being without sin. And before the Fall of *Adam* there was no place for this Covenant, as touching the latter part of the condition; as I presume you will not deny: only the confusion of these two states, before the Fall and after the Fall, hath brought forth this wild conceit of such a Covenant (113, 65–6).

Twisse is not denying that God made a covenant with Adam, only that it was 'in such sort conditionate' as to include obedience and repentance as alternative conditions. Neither does he call into question the basic scheme of the two Covenants of Works and of Grace, for he himself relies on that scheme constantly in his critique of Cotton. The extent of his departure from Federal orthodoxy is that he would evidently separate the full Covenant of Works from the command to Adam and have it go into effect only after the Fall. Perry Miller, however, quotes this passage ('there never was any such Covenant of God with man; I mean, in such sort conditionate . . .') to show that Twisse, having 'the strong theological stomach of the sixteenth century', protested 'frantically' against the very idea of God's making a covenant with man (72, 405).

VI

THE PAULINE RENAISSANCE

PURITANISM is a *commentaire vécu* on the Bible. Its conflicts, dilemmas, and paradoxes are those of the Bible itself, newly apprehended in an age and clime far removed from those in which the book came into being, informing the personal and social consciousness of that later time, and—what is most significant—resuming the process of development. In assimilating the Pauline message that the profound antinomies of the world into which Christ came are reconciled in Christ, sixteenth- and seventeenth-century Puritans realize those antinomies anew in the conditions of their own world.

At the very heart of Puritanism is the subtle but radical antinomy of the scriptural sense of response to God's word and the rational sense of conformity to God's truth. It is only by finding in the Bible, especially in the Epistles of Paul, the fulfillment of the need to reconcile these two senses of obedience to God that Puritans in effect discover that need. When called upon to define it in general, logical terms, abstracted from its specific fulfillment in their experience of the Bible, they flounder. All they manage to say is that their opponents' formula of 'nothing repugnant to scripture', though logically impeccable, is 'not enough'. Yet the conception of Church order which emerges from the complex of Pauline 'rules' concerning edification is indeed as rational and variable, as free from literalism, as the Puritans say it is, and at the same time it is pervasively, even minutely responsive to scriptural direction. It affirms the nomothetic understanding of God's created order, yet it calls the emerging moments of experience into unique relation with the historical revelation of Christ. For those 'rules' do not operate as legal precepts but as imperative indicators of a process: the continual coming into being and perfection of the communal body of Christ, the progressive realization in the life of the Church of a kind of meaning which it would be idle to seek outside the Bible.

Since Church polity is the originally constitutive matter of the

Puritan movement, the Puritans' way of reading the texts on Christian liberty and edification from which they derive their idea of the Church may be taken to indicate that which is distinctive in their approach to scripture. To such readers, Luther's dictum—familiar to English Protestants through Tyndale, who translated Luther's Prologue to Romans and placed it in his English New Testament—that the Epistle to the Romans is 'a light and a way in unto the whole scripture' would mean that the whole Bible has a self-determining unity illuminated by the Epistles of Paul, and everything in it means what it does by virtue of its function in the developing experience of participation in the death and new life of Christ. The Bible is *sui generis*, describable indeed in terms of the general categories of grammar, logic, and rhetoric, but also generating its own principles of order. The Conformist adjusts scripture admirably to the general fabric of 'right discourse', but in doing so he flattens it out, so to speak, producing instead of the dynamic unity of a unique transformation of experience simply the expository unity of a 'doctrinal instrument'.

While the Puritans respond to the element of special obligation implied in Paul's appeal to scripture, their Bible differs in one all-important respect from scripture as Paul understood it: their scripture includes the Gospel and the preaching of Paul himself. The new life in Christ which Paul preached as the end of scripture is now itself conveyed by scripture. The transforming sense of participation in Christ which came to Paul out on an open road, and appeared as the end, in a double sense, of revelation in the written word, now comes ordinarily through the reading of the written word. What the original Disciples knew in the bodily presence of Christ, and Paul in the special apparition of Christ to him, is now ordinarily to be known through the scriptural communication of Christ; '. . . for he is the same in his word, that he was then in bodily presence, the writing of the Apostles do paint him out truly, and nothing but him.'[1] The Puritan can be said to believe in the 'real presence' of Christ in the Bible. The preaching of the word is the original sacrament of Puritanism, without which the Lord's Supper itself is a dead ritual:

And seeing the elements of the world, of which the outward part of the sacraments is taken, be dead and beggarly of themselves, except they be

[1] 42, 76.

animated and enriched with the promise and word of God, which is the life of the Sacraments: what can it be better than sacrilege to separate the ministration of preaching of the word from the sacraments?[2]

Thus both the Old Law from which Christ freed men and the participation in Christ which constitutes their new freedom are now to be found in scripture. Christian liberty does not 'shut out' the word of God, but transforms the experience of the word. Conversion to faith in Christ takes the form of the reapprehension of the scriptures in their vital Pauline unity; it might be called a unique 'literary' experience. Its prototype is to be seen not so much in Paul's experience on the road to Damascus as in Luther's hard-won discovery of how to read certain crucial phrases in the Epistle to the Romans:

Night and day I pondered until I saw the connection between the justice of God and the statement that 'the just shall live by his faith.' Then I grasped that the justice of God is that righteousness by which through grace and sheer mercy God justifies us through faith. Thereupon I felt myself to be reborn and to have gone through open doors into paradise. The whole of Scripture took on a new meaning. . . .[3]

Freedom from the letter involves an unprecedented kind of absorption of mind and personality in the reading of the Bible. Thus faith is bound up with scripture in a way that Paul himself could never have foreseen, even though it evolves out of his work.

When the Puritan says that 'the word of God directeth a man in all his actions', he is insisting that the transformation of life which he finds in the Bible as he reads it should extend throughout the whole range of experience. Nevertheless, a great part of what anyone does in the course of a day is bound to belong to 'the body of this death' which is all there is apart from life in Christ. The Christian warfare on earth is the struggle against this death. The assurance of faith does not mean the end of that warfare. The sins of the elect are 'covered' by Christ, but what the Reformers call 'sanctification' normally goes on throughout a lifetime. As John Cotton describes it, 'sanctification' is the same as 'edification':

There is growth in grace, this sanctification is not bedrid, Christians are not as weak now, as they were seven years ago, nor do they stand at a stay, but go forward in Christianity; and hereupon the Apostle ex-

[2] 43, 61.
[3] 3, 65.

horteth the Ephesians, Chap. 4.15. *To speak the truth in love, that they may grow up into him in all things which is the head, even Christ*: Implying, that men that enter into the ways of holiness ought to grow on unto perfection in the fear of God, *Job. 17.9.* And many sweet means the Lord hath appointed for this end; the communion of God's people tendeth hereto, *Prov. 13.20. He that walketh with the wise, shall learn wisdom.* All the Ordinances of God are appointed for this end, also, to beget and increase Faith and holiness; therefore a Christian in the use of all these Ordinances, doth not stand at a stay, but is still thriving and growing, and that not in his own strength, but in the strength of *Jesus Christ*, seeking for his acceptance and help in every duty he goeth about; and this is that the Apostle doth exhort the *Colossians* unto, Chap. 2.6.7. [As ye have therefore received Christ Jesus the Lord, so walk ye in him: Rooted and built up in him and stabilised in the faith, as ye have been taught, abounding therein with thanksgiving.][4]

Long after the vestiarian controversy has subsided Cotton evokes from the familiar texts on edification the original Puritan sense of what obedience to the word means. It is not a static legalism, for when he says that Christians do not 'stand at a stay' Cotton does not mean that they keep trying harder and succeeding better in obedience to a difficult set of precepts; he means that 'all the Ordinances of God' help Christians to 'grow up into him in all things which is the head, even Christ'. What Cotton says here of the use of God's ordinances might be extended to the use of all parts of God's word. It is a constant growth in which the Bible itself is progressively taken up into that life of Christ which is its true meaning and end. 'If thou wouldest abound in grace', John Preston urges,

. . . study the Scriptures, much attend to them, much meditate in them day and night, labour still to get some new spark of knowledge, some new light out of them, and thou shalt find this, that grace will follow, as it is the Apostle's exhortation to *Timothy*, saith he, *Give attendance to reading, and to learning, so shalt thou save thyself, and shalt be able also to save others.* The meaning is, the way to get that grace that will save a man, is to give much attendance to reading and to learning; for, beloved, whatsoever it is that begets a man, the increase of that likewise edifies and builds him up further. First, *we are begotten by the Word of truth*: it is the revelation of the truth of GOD to a man at the first, that *renews him in the spirit of his mind*; it changeth his judgement, it makes

4 26, 165–6.

him think of things in a clean other fashion than he was wont to do; thus he is begotten to GOD, and made a new man, a new creature. Now the increase of the same truth is it that builds us up further, for whatsoever begets, the increase of that also edifies. . . .[5]

In sum, the idea of participation through the Bible in the new life of Christ underlies the Puritan's appeal to scripture. It explains his otherwise quite baffling insistence that 'there is a word of God for all things we have to do', and it defines his concept of a Church polity 'grounded of the word of God'.

This dynamically Christocentric apprehension of the Bible is the originally distinctive element of Puritanism. To be sure, the Puritans are not the first to take up the Pauline description of the Church as the Body of Christ; nor is it anything new to say that the Bible possesses a unity altogether different in kind from that of any other book. That is the basic principle of medieval exegesis:

Omnis Scriptura divina unus liber est, et ille unus liber Christus est, quia omnis Scriptura divina de Christo loquitur, et omnis Scriptura divina in Christo impletur.[6]

This unity in Christ had always been what was meant, essentially, by the 'spiritual sense' of the scriptures, and to perceive it had even been spoken of as the 'conversion' of the scriptures to Christ.[7] Moreover, where this sense of a text was expounded before its moral meaning, the result, in principle at least, was to affirm that morality drawn from scripture is a further unfolding of the mystery of Christ in the lives of believers. In short, medieval exegesis always was fundamentally Pauline. But Pauline principles take on a new dimension of life in the kind of apprehension of the Bible that is illustrated by Puritan pronouncements on edification. Medieval usage of phrases like *aedificatio morum* and *aedificatio doctrinae* conveys no such idea of dynamic interaction among the members of Christ's body, or of the imperative of life and growth in each member, as the Puritans find in Paul's discussions of the use of idolothytes.[8] Indeed, the Puritan understanding of this complex of terms appears to contrast with medieval usage, just as

---

[5] 91, 449–50.
[6] Hugues de Saint-Victor, *De arca Noe mor.*, I. II, c. viii (*Patrilogia Latina*, CLXXVI, 642 C), quoted by Henri de Lubac (64, 1re Partie, 322).
[7] 64, 1re Partie, 354–5 and 547–8.
[8] 64, 1re Partie, 522–6, and *passim*.

it does with that of Anglican Conformists, who may thus be said to have reverted to the traditional treatment of these themes when challenged by the implications which Puritanism found in them.

By the same token, this Puritan discovery may seem to have been without sequel, for it can hardly be said to have left a trace in later-day usage of the key terms in the Pauline complex of edification and Christian liberty. That fact both registers and in large measure accounts for the success of Whitgift and Hooker in establishing the case for Conformity. Yet the aspect of Puritanism thus obscured from modern view bears a suggestive analogy with a pervasively modern intellectual motif. The Puritan conception of ecclesiastic order as opposed to civil (or 'carnal') order anticipates the influential modern metaphor of 'organic' order as opposed to order which is merely 'mechanical' or 'artificial'. For what is characteristically modern in the use of the organic metaphor does not simply reflect the observation that organic creatures—vegetable or animal—display intricately functional form; it does not consist simply in the habit of comparing social organization or human artifacts to forms of organic nature; nor does the notion that the cosmos itself is an animate creature underlie the distinctively modern—that is, Romantic—metaphor of organic order. All these uses of the metaphor abound in classical antiquity, but the distinctive aspect of the modern usage is the conviction that some instances of order are indeed organic—hence, good—while others, which may well be much like them in appearance, are artificial, mechanical, not good. We may be tempted to read this contradistinction back into classical accounts of well-ordered society or of artistic unity, but it is not there. When ancient writers compare the social order to an organism, they do not do so for the purpose of setting that order off against a social order considered inorganic, but merely to insist on the need for order *tout court*. Our acceptation of the idea of organic order, however, inescapably implies that contrast. Even when the contrast is not expressed, or not even clearly present to the mind of the speaker, it continues to colour our usage of the word 'organic' by imparting to it an honorific value, a 'plus' valence, an overtone of militancy in the great cause of life. This distinctive use of the metaphor to set off a kind of order which is to be approved against another kind which is to be condemned cannot be found in the classical sources from which Romantic theorists are said to have derived their interest in the idea of organic order,[9] but Puritans developed something very like it when they set the kind of communal order they found in Paul over against the kind of order they saw in the Anglican Church as by law established.

Puritanism as a distinct and militant movement within the Anglican Church originates, then, in concern for the communal aspect of Christian experience and is inspired by the vision of an ecclesiastical order which might be characterized as 'organic' in the full, later-day sense of the word. The original character of Elizabethan Puritanism and of seventeenth-century Separatism and Congregationalism bears little relation to the kind of thing which is likely to be suggested by the stock association of Puritanism with 'individualism'. 'The theology of the founders conceived of man as single and alone'—so goes a later-day reconstruction,— 'apart in a corner or in an empty field, wrestling with his sins; only after he had survived this experience in solitude could he walk into the church and by telling about it prove his right to the covenant.'[10] To judge by their writings, 'the founders' habitually conceived of men in congregations rather, and expected faith to come to them normally by the hearing of the word in church—even in an 'implicitly' covenanted Anglican church if true doctrine was preached there. However, the whole question of what constitutes 'the conversion experience' occupies Puritan writers very little in the early period,[11] while the ceaseless nurture and growth of faith within the Church is their incessant theme. As they understand that process, it is all but inconceivable *extra ecclesiam*.

However, that Puritanism was, as the stock idea suggests, conducive to a strong consciousness of individual identity seems all

[9] See M. H. Abrams, *The Mirror and the Lamp: Romantic Theory and the Critical Tradition* (New York, 1953), 184-5.

[10] 69, 160.

[11] The analysis of the process of conversion first becomes a prominent topic of Puritan thought in the work of such men as Richard Rogers, Arthur Hildersam, William Perkins, and Richard Sibbes (see Norman Pettit (89)). That is to say, it emerges in those quarters where the original Puritan insistence on the unique communal nature of the Church has been set aside. Later, as Edmund S. Morgan has shown (77, 93-9), the 'morphology of conversion' formulated by these men comes to figure importantly in Congregational Church polity by providing criteria for the confessions of spiritual experience which come to be required of those seeking membership in the Church. However, the Congregational idea of the Church does not derive fundamentally from this tradition, but from the tradition which leads back, through the early Separatists, to the communal Puritanism of the first part of Elizabeth's reign.

the more probable in view of the special nature of its basic communal conception. Perhaps the Puritans' apprehension of the imperative force of Paul's concept of Christian liberty may be related to the kind of historic cultural crisis in which recent psychological and sociological thought has come to be acutely interested;[12] perhaps, that is, the Puritans' concern to free conscience from whatever has charmed, bound, and sustained it apart from Christ may be related to a developing emancipation of men's consciousness of identity, a developing premonition that cultural configurations which have supported that consciousness in the past can do so now only at the price of intolerably constricting it. In itself, such an emancipation has its dangers, as the modern world has become terribly aware. The false kind of edification against which Paul warns, the mere disengagement of conscience by the knowledge which 'puffeth up', may well call to mind for the modern reader that sorry estrangement of the individual which is the theme of so much anxiety today. But Christian liberty as Paul conceives it, and the Puritans after him, knits individual conscience to communal consciousness indissolubly. Indeed, the interrelation which Puritans insist on between Christian liberty and edification expresses with remarkable clarity the principle that individual identity comes about only through social relationship; but at the same time it defines a social organism which itself arises uniquely from the process of growth in spiritual freedom in its members. This conception of corporate Christian experience, discovered in the struggle against the 'scenic apparatus' of medieval worship, may well have helped to form a sense of individual identity which would not be lost in 'a country without a sovereign, without a court, without a nobility, without an army, without a church or clergy, without a diplomatic service, without a picturesque peasantry'.[13]

Those classes among whom this communal aspect of Puritanism especially flourished may well have resembled, in their uneasy cultural condition, the people to whom Paul had especially addressed himself in the busy, cosmopolitan port-cities of the Mediterranean world. The restless interest in new cults which characterized those mingled urban populations certainly suggests

[12] 39.
[13] *The Notebooks of Henry James*, ed. F. O. Matthiessen and Kenneth B. Murdock (New York, 1947), p. 14.

a prevailing sense of inadequate or lost cultural identity, and it was probably not only the monotheism and high ethical development of Judaism that drew Gentile 'God fearers' to the synagogues, but also the impressive coherence of the life which centred there. To be 'grafted' onto that strong stem, even while indulging a sense of superiority over its old peculiarities, was clearly an appealing idea to many—hence Paul's care to explain the true meaning of both community and freedom in Christ. His explanations would lose much of their bearing in the different kind of world in which Christianity developed over the centuries that followed, but they would speak anew to the very condition of many in the time of the Reformation in England.

Once the Church has come to be conceived of essentially in terms of these Pauline formulations, a problem comes to the fore which was latent in Paul's theology of the Church from the beginning. Paul emphatically does not consider that the Christian community, created by the present work of the Spirit, supersedes the historical people of God, existing by and for the temporal transmission of God's special promise. The seed of Abraham is Christ; the way of thinking by which the people are identified with the single figure of the patriarch is not set aside in favour of the conception of the community as the living body of Christ; somehow the two principles of corporate identity are to be seen as one. The problem of combining these conceptions comes to centre on baptism, which is both the sacrament of union with Christ in his death and resurrection and the seal of belonging to the true seed of the promise.[14] To reject infant baptism is to assert that the Church's identity is solely that of a process in the present. It is to say that the Church transcends secular continuity: there is only one generation in Christ. To baptize infants, on the other hand, is to assert the secular identity of the Church with the apparently

[14] Paul calls circumcision the seal of the covenant with Abraham (Rom. 4:11) and uses the verb 'to seal' in passages where 'it seems almost certain that the word is to be understood as a reference to baptism' (Flemington (41, 66), referring to 2 Cor. 1:21–2, Eph. 1:13–14, and Eph. 4:30). This usage at least strongly suggests that Paul's conception of baptism includes an analogy with circumcision. An analogy, of course, is not a total correspondence, and arguments such as those presented by H. H. Rowley (99, 133–47) do not refute 'the alleged analogy' altogether, but only some points of correspondence. The analogy can be without correspondence in terms of the relation between personal faith and external instrumentality, and yet be significant in terms of the relation between two conceptions of corporate 'belonging'.

inescapable consequence of making the present process of communal life in Christ less than essential to the Church's actual being. Congregational polity denies this consequence, however, asserting for the Church both the historical reality implied by infant baptism and existence by the uniquely present, spontaneous life of the Spirit.

Congregationalism thus undertakes to live by a vital inconsistency answering to the fundamental two-sidedness of Paul's theology of the Church. That ambiguity is implicit from the beginning in that the covenant by which Congregationalists come together to form a church is not accompanied by baptism, where, as is usually the case, those who enter into it have been baptized as infants. That baptism is acknowledged as sealing them inalienably to the historic lineage of God's people, which is the Church; yet until they covenant together for communal profession of the new life that is in them, they are no church. This paradox is not resolved in the writings of Congregational apologists; rather, it is elaborated in relation to the whole, comprehensive pattern of contrasting and yet interinvolved covenants which the Federal Theology comes to trace throughout the biblical account of Creation and the history of man's salvation. Thereby it comes to be seen as an instance of the greatest ambiguity of all: the relation between God's grace and man's response.

Federal Theology develops from the historical and strictly scriptural aspect of Paul's argument for man's dependence on grace. It takes up his account of the historical relation between two contrasting covenants into which God has called his people and finds in the two of them together the basic scheme of creation and redemption. Relations between God and his creatures, between Church and State, between the truly elect and the company of visible saints, between successive economies in the history of the work of redemption, between unmerited grace and good works, all come to be described in terms of Covenants elaborating the interaction between those two great Covenant traditions. The whole of experience, universal and personal, in nature, in history, in grace itself, is seen to be structured upon that biblical dialectic. Federal Theology works outward from Paul to a comprehensive, coherent, and cogent understanding of the Bible and thereby of all things visible and invisible. It bids fair to be the ultimate achievement of Reformation biblical theology.

By remaining loyally attentive to the Bible and to human experience, Federal Theology incurs the suspicion of those who have come to focus their thought on the abstract principle of God's sovereignty and to regard it as the whole duty of theology to maintain the non-historical, inconceivable, but logically indispensable postulate of predestination. Any discussion which dwells on the relation between justice and grace in actual human experience and in the biblical account is likely to make such insistent predestinarians uneasy, as though it threatened at any moment to begin justifying God's ways to himself. It is this desiccated orthodoxy itself, however, and not Federal Theology, which represents a devolution from the thought of the great sixteenth-century reformers in the matter of predestination.

Federal Theology does contribute to a change in the quality of Reformed Christianity, but one of a very different kind, which the notion of Federalism as essentially a system of equivocation on the point of predestination has obscured. In developing the aspect of Pauline theology which is a reinterpretation of scriptural tradition in its own terms, Federalism tends to neglect the other aspect, that which describes the experience of grace as participation in Christ. At the same time, by its tendency to suggest that assurance is to be found in observable signs of sanctification as Covenant 'conditions' evidencing others, Federalism appears to warrant a kind of 'sacramental system' of good works. But as good works themselves are only as good as the spiritual 'motions' which they manifest, to seek assurance from Covenant 'conditions' is inevitably to become much concerned with emotional experiences, to assess their spiritual value attentively and to put trust in those that are true. Thus, where the figure of Christ has become dim, and the Pauline phrases about participating in Christ by the Spirit have become more or less otiose formulas, a religion of 'religious experience' may develop within the Federalist frame in place of Paul's 'Christ mysticism'.

This development may be called the last phase of the Pauline Renaissance. It is roughly last in point of time, becoming conspicuous in the decades following the failure of the Elizabethan Puritan movement; and it represents, not a further realization, but a dissolution of the Pauline synthesis. It brings to an end the history of Puritanism as a working out of the faith that all things come together in Christ.

BIBLIOGRAPHY

1. AINSWORTH, HENRY. *The Communion of Saincts*. Reprinted, 1615.
2. AMES, WILLIAM. *The Marrow of Sacred Divinity*. London, n.d.
3. BAINTON, ROLAND H. *Here I Stand: A life of Martin Luther*. New York, 1950.
4. BALL, JOHN. *A Tryall of the New-Church Way in New-England and in Old*. London. 1644.
5. BANCROFT, RICHARD. *Tracts Ascribed to Richard Bancroft*, ed. Albert Peel. Cambridge, England, 1953.
6. [BARROW, HENRY]. *A True Description out of the Word of God of the Visible Church*. 1610.
7. BEST, ERNEST. *One Body in Christ: A Study in the Relationship of the Church to Christ in the Epistles of the Apostle Paul*. London (Society for the Propagation of Christian Knowledge), 1955.
8. BLAKE, THOMAS. *Vindiciae Foederis; or a Treatise of the Covenant of God Entered With Man-kinde*. London, 1653.
9. BRADSHAW, WILLIAM. *A Treatise of the Nature and Use of Things Indifferent*. 1605.
10. BRIDGES, JOHN. *A Defence of the government established in the Church of Englande for ecclesiastical matters*. London, 1587.
11. BROOK, V. J. K. *Whitgift and the English Church*. London, 1957.
12. BROWN, RAYMOND E., trans. and ed. *The Gospel according to John* (The Anchor Bible, vol. 29). Garden City, 1966.
13. BROWNE, ROBERT. *The Writings of Robert Harrison and Robert Browne*, ed. Albert Peel and Leland H. Carlson. London, 1953.
14. BULKELEY, PETER. *The Gospel-Covenant; . . .* 2nd edn., London, 1615.
15. CALVIN, JOHN. *The Institutes of Christian Religion*, trans. Ford L. Battles, ed. John T. McNeil. 2 vols., Philadelphia, 1960.
16. CARTWRIGHT, THOMAS. *Cartwrightiana*, ed. Albert Peel and Leland Carlson. London, 1951.
17. CARTWRIGHT, THOMAS. *The Second Replie of Thomas Cartwright: Agaynst Maister Doctor Whitgiftes Second Answer, Touching the Church Discipline*, 1575.
18. CERFAUX, L. *The Church in the Theology of St. Paul*, trans. Geoffrey Webb and Adrian Walker. New York and London, 1959; original French publication Paris, 1947.
19. CHERRY, CONRAD. *The Theology of Jonathan Edwards: A Reappraisal*. New York [unsewn], 1966.

20. CLEBSH, WILLIAM A. *England's Earliest Protestants*. New Haven and London, 1964.
21. COLLINSON, PATRICK. *The Elizabethan Puritan Movement*. London and Berkeley and Los Angeles, 1967.
22. COTTON, JOHN. *Certain Queries Tending to Accommodation and Communion of Presbyterian and Congregational Churches*. London, 1654.
23. COTTON, JOHN. *The Covenant of God's free Grace*. London, 1645.
24. COTTON, JOHN. *Gospel Conversion*. . . . London, 1646.
25. COTTON, JOHN. *The Grounds and Ends of the Baptisme of the Children of the Faithfull*. London, 1647.
26. COTTON, JOHN. *The New Covenant*, . . . London, 1654.
27. COTTON, JOHN. *Of the Holinesse of Church-Members*. London, 1650.
28. COTTON, JOHN. *The Way of Congregational Churches Cleared*. London, 1648.
29. COURVOISIER, JACQUES. *La Notion d'église chez Bucer dans son développement historique*. Paris, 1933.
30. CRANFIELD, C. E. B. *The Gospel According to St. Mark* (The Cambridge Greek Testament Commentary). Cambridge, England [unsewn], 1963.
31. [CROWLEY, ROBERT]. *A briefe discourse against the outwarde apparell and Ministring garmentes of the popishe church*. 1566.
32. DE JONG, PETER. *The Covenant Idea in New England Theology, 1620–1847*. Grand Rapids, Michigan, 1945.
33. DICKENS, A. G. *The English Reformation*. New York [unsewn], n.d.; first published London, 1964.
34. DOWNAME, JOHN. *The Christian Warfare*. London, 1608.
35. DOWNAME, GEORGE. *The Covenant of Grace* . . . Dublin, 1631.
36. EMERSON, EVERETT, H. 'Calvin and Covenant Theology', *Church History*, XXV, no. 2 (June 1956), 136–44.
37. EMERSON, EVERETT H. *John Cotton*. New York, 1965.
38. ERASMUS. *In Pauli Apostoli Epistolas* . . . *Paraphrasis*, ed. Deichmann. Hanover, n.d.
39. ERIKSON, ERIK H. *Childhood and Society*. New York, 1950; revised edn., 1963.
40. EUSDEN, JOHN D. *Puritans, Lawyers, and Politics in Early Seventeenth-Century England*. New Haven, 1958.
41. FLEMINGTON, W. F. *The New Testament Doctrine of Baptism*. London (Society for Promoting Christian Knowledge), 1948.
42. FRERE, W. H. and DOUGLAS, C. E., ed. *Puritan Manifestoes: A Study of the Origin of the Puritan Revolt*. London (Society for Promoting Christian Knowledge, Church Historical Society Publication LXXII), 1907.

43. [FULKE, WILLIAM]. *A Brief and plaine declaration, concerning the desires of all those faithfull Ministers, that have and do seeke for the Discipline and reformation of the church of Englande. Which may serve for a just Apologie, against the false accusations and slaunders of their adversaries.* London, 1584. (Often called by its subtitle *A Learned Discourse.*)

44. GÄRTNER, BERTIL. *The Temple and the Community in Qumran and the New Testament: A Comparative Study in the Temple Symbolism of the Qumran Texts and the New Testament.* Cambridge, England, 1965.

45. GATAKER, THOMAS. *A Mistake, or Misconstruction, Removed.* London, 1646.

46. GEORGE, CHARLES H. and KATHARINE. *The Protestant Mind of the English Reformation.* Princeton, 1961.

47. GEREE, JOHN. *Vindiciae Paedo-Baptismi.* London, 1646.

48. [GILBY, ANTHONY]. *A Pleasaunt Dialogue, Betweene a Souldior of Barwicke, and an English Chaplaine.* . . . 1581.

49. GOODWIN, JOHN. *Imputatio Fidei.* London, 1642.

50. HALLER, WILLIAM. *The Rise of Puritanism.* New York, 1938.

51. HARNACK, ADOLPH. *History of Dogma,* trans. Neil Buchanan. New York, 1961.

52. HATCH, EDWIN. *The Influence of Greek Ideas on Christianity.* London, 1888; New York [unsewn], 1957.

53. HEADLEY, JOHN M. *Luther's View of Church History.* New Haven and London, 1963.

54. HERBERT, GEORGE. *The Works of George Herbert,* ed. F. L. Hutchinson. Oxford, 1941.

55. HILL, CHRISTOPHER. *Society and Puritanism in Pre-Revolutionary England.* New York, 1964.

56. HOLL, KARL. 'Der Kirchenbegriff des Paulus in seinem Verhältnis zu dem der Urgemeinde' (1921), in *Gesammelte Aufsätze zur Kirchengeschichte,* II. (First issued Tübingen, 1928) Darmstadt, 1964. pp. 44–67.

57. HOOKER, RICHARD. *Works,* ed. John Keble. 3 vols., Oxford, 1874.

58. HOPF, CONSTANTIN, *Martin Bucer and the English Reformation.* Oxford, 1956.

59. JEWEL, JOHN. *Works,* ed. John Ayre. Cambridge, England, 1845.

60. JUSTIN. *Dialogue with Trypho,* trans. A. Lukyn Williams. London (Society for Promoting Christian Knowledge), 1930.

61. KNAPPEN, M. M. *Tudor Puritanism.* Chicago, 1939.

62. [LAMBARDE, WILLIAM]. *A Defense of the Ecclesiasticall Regiment in Englande, defaced by T.C. in his Replie agaynst D. Whitgifte.* London, 1574.

63. LÉONARD, EMILE G. *A History of Protestantism: The Reformation*, trans. Joyce M. H. Reid, ed. H. H. Rowley. London, 1965; original French publication Paris, 1961.

64. de LUBAC, HENRI. *Exégèse médiévale: les quatre sens de l'écriture*. 4 vols., Paris, 1959–64.

65. McCOY, CHARLES S. 'Johannes Cocceius: Federal Theologian', *Scottish Journal of Theology*, XVI (1963).

66. McGINN, DONALD J. *The Admonition Controversy*. New Brunswick, 1949.

67. MARSHALL, STEPHEN. *A Sermon for the Baptizing of Infants*. London, 1644.

68. MENDENHALL, GEORGE E. *Law and Covenant in Israel and the Ancient Near East*. Pittsburgh, 1955; reprinted from *The Biblical Archeologist*, XVII, nos. 2 and 3 (May and September 1954).

69. MILLER, PERRY. *Errand into the Wilderness*. Cambridge, Mass., 1956.

70. MILLER, PERRY. *Jonathan Edwards*. New York, 1949.

71. MILLER, PERRY. *The New England Mind: From Colony to Province*. Cambridge, Mass., 1953.

72. MILLER, PERRY. *The New England Mind: The Seventeenth Century*. Cambridge, Mass., 1939; reissued 1954.

73. MILLER, PERRY. *Orthodoxy in Massachusetts, 1630–1650*. Boston [unsewn], 1959; first published Cambridge, Mass., 1933.

74. MÖLLER, GRETE. 'Föderalismus und Geschichtsbetrachtung im XVII. und XVIII. Jahrhundert', *Zeitschrift für Kirchengeschichte*, Dritte Folge, I, L. Band, Heft III/IV (1931), 393–440.

75. MØLLER, JENS G. 'The Beginnings of Puritan Covenant Theology', *The Journal of Ecclesiastical History*, XIV, no. 1 (April 1963), 46–67.

76. MORGAN, EDMUND S. *The Puritan Family: Religion and Domestic Relations in Seventeenth-Century New England*. New York [unsewn], 1966; first published Boston, 1944.

77. MORGAN, EDMUND S. *Visible Saints: The History of a Puritan Idea*. New York, 1963.

78. MUNCK, JOHANNES, trans. and ed. *The Acts of the Apostles*, revised by William F. Albright and C. S. Mann (The Anchor Bible, Bible, vol. 31). Garden City, 1967.

79. NEW, JOHN F. H. *Anglican and Puritan: The Bases of Their Opposition 1558–1640*. Stanford, 1964.

80. NEWMAN, MURRAY LEE, Jr. *The People of the Covenant: A Study of Israel from Moses to the Monarchy*. New York and Nashville, 1962.

81. NUTTALL, GEOFFREY F. *Visible Saints: The Congregational Way, 1640–1660*. Oxford, 1957.

82. ORIGEN. 'Commentariorum in Evangelium Secundum Joannem', *Patrologica Graeca*, ed. J. P. Migne. XIV (1857).

83. PARKER, MATTHEW. *A brief examination for the tyme, of a certaine declaration, lately put in print in the name and defence of certaine Ministers in London, refusyng to weare the apparell prescribed by the lawes and orders of the Realme. . . .* n.d.

84. *A parte of a register, contayning sundrie memorable matters, written by divers godly and learned in our time, which stande for and desire the reformation of our Church, in Discipline and Ceremonies, accordinge to the pure worde of God, and the Lawe of our Lande.* n.d. ('A godly and zealous letter written by Mai. A.G. 1570'.)

85. PEDERSEN, JOHANNES. *Israel: Its Life and Culture.* trans. Aslaug Møller. London and Copenhagen, reprinted 1959; first published 1926.

86. [PERKINS, WILLIAM]. *A Briefe discourse, taken out of the writings of Her. Zanchius. . . .* London, 1595.

87. PERKINS, WILLIAM. *A Case of Conscience, the greatest that ever was; How a man may know whether he be the Childe of God, or no.* London, 1595.

88. PERKINS, WILLIAM. *Works.* Cambridge, England, 1600.

89. PETTIT, NORMAN. *The Heart Prepared: Grace and Conversion in Puritan Spiritual Life.* New Haven and London, 1966.

90. PFAMMATTER, JOSEPH. *Die Kirche Als Bau: Eine exegetisch-theologishe Studie zur Ekklesiolgie der Paulusbriefe.* Rome, 1960.

91. Preston, John. *The New Covenant, or The Saints Portion.* 5th edn., London, 1630.

92. PRESTON, JOHN. *Paul's Conversion. . . .* London, 1637.

93. ROBINSON, HASTINGS, ed. *The Zurich Letters.* Cambridge, England (Parker Society), 1842.

94. ROBINSON, H. WHEELER. 'The Hebrew Conception of Corporate Personality', *Werden und Wesen des Alten Testaments; Beiheft zur Zeitschrift für die alttestamentliche Wissenschaft*, ed. J. Hempel. 1936. pp. 49–62.

95. VON ROHR, JOHN. 'The Congregationalism of Henry Jacob', *Transactions of The Congregational Historical Society*, XIX, no. 3 (October, 1962), 107–22.

96. VON ROHR, JOHN. 'Covenant Assurance in Early English Puritanism', *Church History*, XXXIV, no. 2 (June 1965), 195–203.

97. VON ROHR, JOHN. '*Extra ecclesiam nulla salus:* An Early Congregational Version', Presidential Address, The American Society of Church History, delivered 29 December 1966.

98. ROWLEY, H. H., ed. *The Old Testament and Modern Study: A Generation of Discovery and Research.* Oxford, 1951.

99. ROWLEY, H. H. *The Unity of the Bible*. New York, 1957; first published London, 1953.

100. SALTMARSH, JOHN. *The Smoke in the Temple*. London, 1646.

101. SALTMARSH, JOHN. *Shadows flying away, in Some Drops of the Viall*, . . . London, 1646.

102. SCHACKENBURG, RUDOLF. *Baptism in the Thought of St. Paul: A Study in Pauline Theology*, trans. G. F. Beasley-Murray. Oxford, 1964.

103. Schoeps, Hans Joachim. *Paul: The Theology of the Apostle in the Light of Jewish Religious History*, trans. Harold Knight. London, 1961; first published in German, Tübingen, 1959.

104. SCHRENK, GOTTLOB. *Gottesreich und Bund im älteren Protestantismus vornehmlich bei Johannes Cocceius*. Gütersloh, 1923.

105. SCHWEITZER, ALBERT. *The Mysticism of Paul the Apostle*, trans. William Montgomery. London, 1931; original publication in German, Tübingen, 1930.

106. SCHWEIZER, EDUARD. *Church Order in the New Testament*, trans. Frank Clarke. London, 1961; original publication in German, Zurich, 1959.

107. SENHOUSE, RICHARD. *Four Sermons Preached at the Court upon severall occasions*. London, 1627.

108. SIBBES, RICHARD. *The Bruised Reed and Smoking Flax*, ed. Alexander Grosart. London, 1862.

109. SIMPSON, ALAN. *Puritanism in Old and New England*. Chicago, 1955.

110. SPEISER, E. A. *Genesis* (The Anchor Bible, vol. 1). Garden City, 1964.

111. TAWNEY, R. H. *Religion and the Rise of Capitalism*. New York, 1926.

112. TRINTERUD, LEONARD J. 'The Origins of Puritanism', *Church History*, XX, no. 1 (March 1951), 35–57.

113. TWISSE, WILLIAM. *A Treatise of Mr. Cottons, Clearing certaine Doubts Concerning Predestination. Together with an Examination Thereof.* . . . London, 1646.

114. DE VAUX, ROLAND. *Ancient Israel*. London, 1965.

115. VIELHAUER, PHILIPP. Oikodome: *Das Bild vom Bau in der christlichen Literatur nom Neuen Testament bis Clemens Alexandrinus*. Karlsruhe-Durlach, 1939.

116. VRIEZEN, TH. C. *The Religion of Ancient Israel*, trans. Hubert Hoskins. London, 1967; original publication in Dutch, Arnhem, 1963.

117. WALKER, WILLISTON. *The Creeds and Platforms of Congregationalism*. Boston, 1960; original edition New York, 1893.

118. WEBER, MAX. *The Protestant Ethic and the Spirit of Capitalism*, trans. Talcott Parsons. New York [unsewn], 1958.

119. WENDEL, FRANÇOIS. *Calvin: The Origins and Development of his Religious Thought*, trans. Philip Mairet. New York, 1963; original publication in French, Paris, 1950.
120. WHITGIFT, JOHN. *The Works of John Whitgift*, ed. John Ayre. 3 vols., Cambridge, England (Parker Society), 1851.
    These volumes also contain the most convenient text of much of Cartwright's work, since Whitgift, in his *Defence of the Answer to the Admonition, Against the Reply of Thomas Cartwright*, reproduces the whole controversy up to that point, quoting Cartwright's statements and his own former replies in their entirety. Quotations from Cartwright which are thus to be found in the Parker Society Whitgift are made from that edition.
121. WINDELBAND, WILHELM. *Geschichte und Naturwissenschaft*. Strassburg, 1894.
122. [WOOD, THOMAS]. *A Brieff discours off the troubles begonne at Franckford in Germany Anno Domini 1554*. [Heidelberg], 1575. (For the probability that this document is by Wood, rather than by William Whittingham, to whom it has traditionally been attributed, see Patrick Collinson, 'The Authorship of *A Brieff Discours off the Troubles Begonne at Franckford*', *The Journal of Ecclesiastical History*, IX, no. 2 (October, 1958), 188–208.)
123. ZIFF, LARZER. *The Career of John Cotton: Puritanism and the American Experience*. Princeton, 1962.

INDEX

The titles of works quoted or referred to in the text are here greatly abbreviated.
For full particulars see the Bibliography

Abrams, M. H., 147 n.
Admonition controversy, 1, 4–11, 127 n.
Ainsworth, Henry, *Communion*, 69, 84, 88
Ames, William, 74 n.; *Marrow*, 66, 67, 108
Antinomianism, 100, 119
Arminianism, 89, 116, 117
assurance of election, 122–7, 131–7, 151
Augustine, 116

Bainton, R. H., *Here*, 143
Baker, Herschel, 6 n.
Ball, John, *Tryall*, 84
Bamcroft, Richard, *Tracts*, 49
baptism: related to circumcision, 84, 149; and generation or regeneration, 84–5; Paul's attitude toward and that of original community, 85–7; of children, 84–6; problem of reconciling two concepts of corporate identity centres on, 86–7, 149
Barrow, Henry, *True Description*, 58 n.
Bartlet, William, 64 n.
Belloc, Hilaire, xii n.
Best, Ernest, *One Body*, 36, 48 n.
Betz, O., 33 n.
Bible: reading of as exodus from realm of images, xii; 'biblical process', xiv, 107; and Puritan thought, xiii, 1–2, 150; 'according to' vs. 'not against', 7–12, 141; unity in diversity of, xiii–xiv, 142; conversion as transformation of, 142–3, 145
Blake, Thomas, *Vindiciae*, 88, 108, 112, 125, 126, 129
Bradshaw, William, *Treatise*, 68
Bridges, John, *Defence*, 1, 7, 45, 55
Brown, R. E., *John*, 13 n.
Browne, Robert, 122; *Writings*, 56, 57, 61, 62, 63, 69, 71, 74, 96, 100, (Harrison) 58, 62

Bucer, Martin, 25 n., 47–8, 60, 72 n.
Bulkeley, Peter, *Gospel-Covenant*, 102–3, 110, 112, 121–2, 123–4, 129, 132, 135
Bullinger, Heinrich, 25 n.

Calvin, John, 115–16; *Institutes*, 43, 55, 82, 83, 90, 92, 121 n., 122, 130, 131, 133–4, 135–6 n.
Cartwright, Thomas, 58, 127; *Cartwrightiana*, 70; *Second Replie*, 3, 5, 10, 11, 24, 50, 52, 57, 115 n.; *see* Whitgift
Cerfaux, L., *Church*, 36 n., 38 n., 48 n., 77 n.
Cherry, Conrad, *Edwards*, 138 n.
Christ: scriptural obedience as captivity to, 18; centrality of for Paul, 30–1, 38, 128–9, 151–2; communal identity in, 34, 36–9; power of creates Church, 61–2, 66–8; obscured in Covenant Theology, 128–131, 137–8, 151–2; participation in through Bible, 141–5
Church: Paul's complex theology of, xiii, 78, 86–7, 93–4, 98, 150; Puritans' four rules for, 5, 52–3, 141; as temple, 33, 35, 36, 38, 47, 50, 52, 74; as body of Christ, 35–9, 48, 50, 61, 62, 67–8, 79, 145; and state, 51–52, 57–8, 69; 'lively', 58, 60; visible and invisible, 73–4, 87–9, 93, 95; temporal dimension of, 77–80, 82–3, 86, 89, 93, 95, 149–50; and family, 83, 94
civil disobedience: Christian liberty necessitates, 26–7, 57
Clebsh, William, *Protestants*, 127 n.
Communist Manifesto, xii
conversion experience: testimony of required for Church membership, 64–6, 147 n.; morphology of, 65–6, 103, 147 n.; preoccupation with not characteristic of early Puritanism, 147

corporate personality, 34, 80–1

Cotton, John: *Queries*, 88, 89; *Covenant*, 84, 131; *Gospel*, 112, 116, 131; *Grounds*, 83, 86, 88, 89–90, 108, 121 n.; *New Covenant*, 90–1, 92–3, 103, 104, 111, 112, 113, 131, 132, 133, 134, 135 n., 137–8, 143–4; *Holiness*, 74; *Way*, 64, 137; *see* Twisse

Courvoisier, Jacques, *Notion*, 72 n.

Covenant, Church: as form of profession, 62–6, 75; makes possible compromise with Established Church, 69–70, 75; implicit, 71, 75; and historical continuity, 80–3; and federal grace, 87–93; renewal of, 96–8; and Covenant Theology, 98, 106, 150

Covenant conditions: absent from Abrahamic Covenant, 100–1; peculiarity of in Mosaic Covenant, 101, 104–5; Mosaic tradition associated with, 106; unreal distinction between small and great, 109–12, 120, 122; ambiguity of, 107–9, 112–13, 120; basis of created order, 108, 119, 121; sequence of, 120–2, 125; quasi-sacramental use of as marks and signs, 126–7, 131–3, 151; introspection for, 132–5

Covenant with Abraham: Paul's argument from, 80–1; unites OT and NT, 81–2; not conditional, 100–1; vs. Mosaic Covenant, 101, 104, 106–107; and continuity of Church, 83; and Covenant of Grace, 102

Covenant with Moses: vs. Abrahamic Covenant, 101, 104, 106–7; peculiar conditionality of, 101, 104–5; and Covenant of Works, 101–2; and Covenant of Nature, 102; and command to Adam, 102–3; and form of suzerainty treaty, 104

Cranfield, C. E. B., *Mark*, 33 n.

Cross, F. L., *Oxford Dictionary of the Christian Church*, 6 n.

Crowley, Robert, 127 n.; *briefe discourse*, 26, 27, 47

de Vaux, Roland, *Ancient Israel*, 28 n.

De Visscher, F., 36 n.

Dickens, A. G., *Reformation*, xii

discipline: as manifesting power of Christ, 60–2; as form of profession, 62–3

Downame, George, *Covenant*, 125, 128

Downame, John, 127; *Warfare*, 124, 125–6, 127, 128

Edwards, Jonathan, 121 n., 138 n.

Erasmus, 14, 111; *Paraphrasis*, 14

Erastianism: Christian liberty basis of in England, 26, 43

Erikson, E. H., *Childhood*, 148

Faerie Queene, xi

Flemington, W. F., *Baptism*, 85 n., 149 n.

Frere, W. H. and Douglas, C. E., *Manifestoes*, xii, 142

Fulke, William, *declaration*, 6, 142–3

Gärtner, Bertil, *Temple*, 31, 32, 33, 34

Gataker, Thomas, *Mistake*, 109

Geree, John, *Vindiciae*, 83, 87

Gilby, Anthony, 127 n.; *Dialogue*, 23, 41 n., 42, 49, 56, 63, 108

Goodwin, John, *Imputatio*, 108

grace: federal, 89–90, 92–3; common graces, 90, 91–3; and predestination, 115–16, 118; uniqueness of as Covenant condition, 118–19

Harnack, Adolph, *Dogma*, 18 n.

Harrison, Robert, *see* Browne

Hatch, Edwin, *Greek Ideas*, 18 n.

Headley, J. M., *Luther's View*, 80 n.

Herbert, George, *Works*, 62, 68

Hildersam, Arthur, 147 n.

Holl, Karl, 'Kirchenbegriff', 33 n.

Hooker, Richard, 1, 4, 9, 22, 146; *Works*, xii, 3, 6, 8, 10, 12, 13, 15, 20, 21, 24 n., 26 n., 53, 58, 75 n.

Hopf, Constantin, *Bucer*, 26 n.

Hugues de Saint-Victor, 145

Humphrey, Laurence, 25 n.

hypocrisy, 88–91

identity: Pauline ecclesiology addressed to problem of, xiii, 147–9; and 'house' in OT, 27–8, 83, 94; of community in Christ, 34–5, 38–41, 80, 86; and historic continuity, 86; two principles of deriving from Exodus, 105–6; Puritanism and individual, 147–9 idiographic vs. nomothetic, 16–17, 34 n., 141

idolatry: death penalty for, 24 n.; as subjection to elements of the world, 47, 97

idolothytes, 23, 41–2, 49, 50, 59

indifferent things: Puritanism emerges out of dispute over, 23–7, 41–7, 63; 'weak and beggarly elements', 39, 50, 51, 56, 142; use of to establish order, 43, 49, 51–2, 56, 63; Perkins discusses edification without reference to, 59–60

James, Henry, 148

Jeremiah, 29–30

Jewel, John, xi, 26 n.; *Works*, 127 n.

Justin, *Trypho*, 19

La Fontaine, 37

Lambarde, William, *Defense*, xiii

Léonard, E. G., *Protestantism*, 115 n.

Locke, 138 n.

Lubac, Henri de, *Exégèse*, 145 n.

Lucretius, 108 n.

Luther, 103, 111, 116, 127, 142, 143

McCoy, C. S., 'Cocceius', 117–18 n.

McGinn, D. J., *Admonition*, 27 n.

Marshall, Stephen, *Sermon*, 86, 87–8

Martyr, Peter, xi n., 43

Mather, Richard, 75 n.

Mendenhall, G. E., *Law*, 104–5, 107

Menenius Agrippa, fable of, 36–7

Miller, Perry, *Errand*, 138, 147; *Edwards*, 121 n.; *New England* (I), 66, 75; (II), 2, 140; *Orthodoxy*, xiii, 6 n., 61, 72 n., 73, 74, 75, 89

Milton, 41

Morgan, E. S., *Saints*, 65 n., 72–3 n., 147 n.

Munck, Johannes, *Acts*, 32 n.

nature: and scripture, 10–15, 21, 103; Covenant of, 102–3, 108 n.

New, J. F. H., *Anglican*, 115 n., 127 n.

Newman, M. L. Jr., *People*, 106 n.

Newton, 121 n., 138 n.

Nuttall, G. F., *Saints*, 64, 65, 66, 70 n., 71, 75, 76

offence to conscience: rule against, 5, 52–3; two kinds of, 42, 50; given vs. taken, 42–3, 50; vs. edification,

51–2; Perkins defines, 59–60; semi-separatist compromise avoids, 70

οἶκος and compounds, 27, 35–6, 41

organic order, 35–41, 47–52, 69, 75, 146–7

Origen, 'in Joannem', 19

Owen, John, 66, 75

Panofsky, Erwin, 16 n., 60 n.

Parker, Matthew, *examination*, 23, 25 n., 41 n., 43, 44, 45, 46

parte of a register, A, 13

Paul: as guide to scripture, xiii, 104, 142, 150; dialectic nature of his thought, xiv, 17, 21, 78, 84, 98, 141, 150; and Christian humanism, 13–14; Jewish and Greek components in his thought, 15, 17, 21, 27, 33–5, 141

Pedersen, Johannes, *Israel*, 28 n., 34 n.

Perkins, William, 127 n., 147 n.; *discourse*, 122–3; *Case of Conscience*, 125; *Works*, 59, 60

Pettit, Norman, *Heart*, 147 n.

Pfammatter, Joseph, *Kirche*, 27 n., 33 n., 48 n.

Phaedo, 77

predestination: and Separatist polity, 72, 74–5, 93; and Calvinism, 115–118; and Covenant Theology, 116–120, 139–40, 151

Preston, John, 120, 127; *New Covenant*, 110, 124, 125, 130–1, 144–5; *Paul's Conversion*, 132

Puritanism: and 'elimination of magic', xi–xii; in what sense based on Bible, 4–6, 9–12, 21–2, 50, 52–4, 75, 141–5; distinctive contribution of to interpretation of Paul, 21, 48–49, 77 n.; divided tradition of, 56–60, 96, 127, 147 n.; and 'individualism', 147–8

Qumran community, 31–5

Richard II, xii

Robinson, Hastings, *Zurich Letters*, xi, 43, 44

Robinson, H. W., *Hebrew Conception*, 81 n.

Rogers, Richard, 147 n.

Rollins, Hyder, 6 n.

Rowley, H. H., *Old Testament*, 80–81 n.; *Unity*, xiii, xiv, 149 n.

sacraments (*see also* baptism): as seals, 84, 89, 149; good works as, 126–7, 131, 151; and preaching of word, 142–3

Saltmarsh, John, 96, 114; *Smoke*, 84, 94–5; *Shadows*, 111

Sampson, Richard, 25 n.

Schackenburg, Rudolf, *Baptism*, 85 n.

Schoeps, H. J., *Paul*, xiv, 80 n.

Schrenk, Gottlob, *Gottesreich*, 102 n.

Schweitzer, Albert, *Mysticism*, 39 n., 80 n.

semi-separatists, 69–76

Senhouse, Richard, 122; *Sermons*, 99–100, 123

Servetus, 81

Sibbes, Richard, 147 n.; *Bruised Reed*, 122

Speiser, E. A., *Genesis*, xiv, 28 n., 100–101

Spiro, Abram, 32 n.

Stephen: and opposition to Temple cult, 32–3

Tawney, R. H., *Religion*, 69

toleration, 64

Travers, Walter, 58, 127 n.

Trinterud, L. J., 'Origins', 127 n.

Twisse, William, *Treatise*, 91, 113–14, 115, 116, 117, 139–40, (Cotton) 91–92, 116–17, 118, 119, 138

Tyndale, William, 127, 142

vestiarian controversy, 23–4, 41–7, 51, 55–6, 63–4

Vielhauer, Philipp, Oikodome, 27 n.

voluntarism, 66–9

Vriezen, Th. C., *Religion*, 106 n.

Walker, Williston, *Creeds*, 68, 97

Weber, Max, *Protestant Ethic*, xi

Whitgift, William, 146; *Works*, 2, 5, 7, 8, 24, 25, 44, (Cartwright) 4, 5, 6, 8, 24, 51, 55, 56

Wilson, John Dover, xii n.

Windelband, Wilhelm, *Geschichte*, 16

Wood, Thomas, *Brieff discours*, 79